My Book of
Stars
AND
Planets

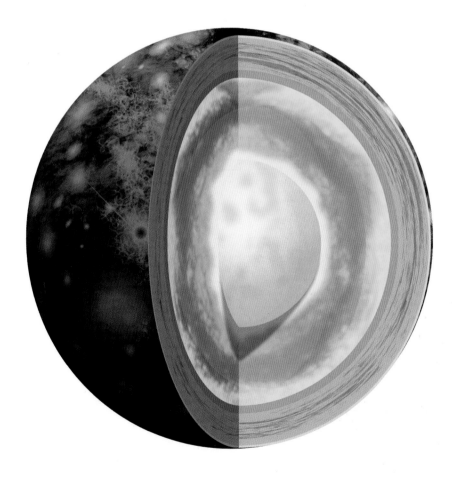

Author: Dr. Parshati Patel

Project editors Manisha Majithia, Kritika Gupta
Editors Katie Lawrence, Joy Evatt
Assistant editor Niharika Prabhakar
US Editor Mindy Fichter
US Senior editor Shannon Beatty
Senior art editors Ann Cannings, Nidhi Mehra
Project art editor Jaileen Kaur
Assistant art editor Aishwariya Chattoraj
Jacket coordinator Issy Walsh
Jacket designer Dheeraj Arora
DTP designers Dheeraj Singh,
Syed Md Farhan
Project picture researcher Sakshi Saluja
Production editor Dragana Puvacic
Production controller John Casey
Managing editors Jonathan Melmoth,
Monica Saigal
Managing art editors Diane Peyton Jones,
Romi Chakraborty
Delhi team heads Glenda Fernandes,
Malavika Talukder
Deputy art director Mabel Chan
Publishing director Sarah Larter

Illustrator Dan Crisp
Consultant Professor David W. Hughes

First American Edition, 2021
Published in the United States by DK Publishing
1745 Broadway, 20th Floor, New York, NY 10019

A catalog record for this book is
available from the Library of Congress
ISBN 978-0-7440-3496-7

DK books are available at special discounts when
purchased in bulk for sales promotions, premiums,
fundraising, or educational use. For details, contact:
DK Publishing Special Markets,
1745 Broadway, 20th Floor, New York, NY 10019
SpecialSales@dk.com

Printed and bound in China

For the curious
www.dk.com

Contents

4 What is space?
6 Looking at the sky
8 Orion constellation
9 Ursa Major constellation
10 Constellations
12 Observatories
14 Our place in space
16 Solar system
18 The sun
20 Mercury
22 Venus
24 Earth
26 The moon
28 Mars
30 Jupiter
32 Jupiter's moons
34 Saturn
36 Saturn's moons
38 Uranus
40 Neptune
42 Pluto
43 Ceres
44 Space rocks
46 Vesta
47 Comet 67P/C-G

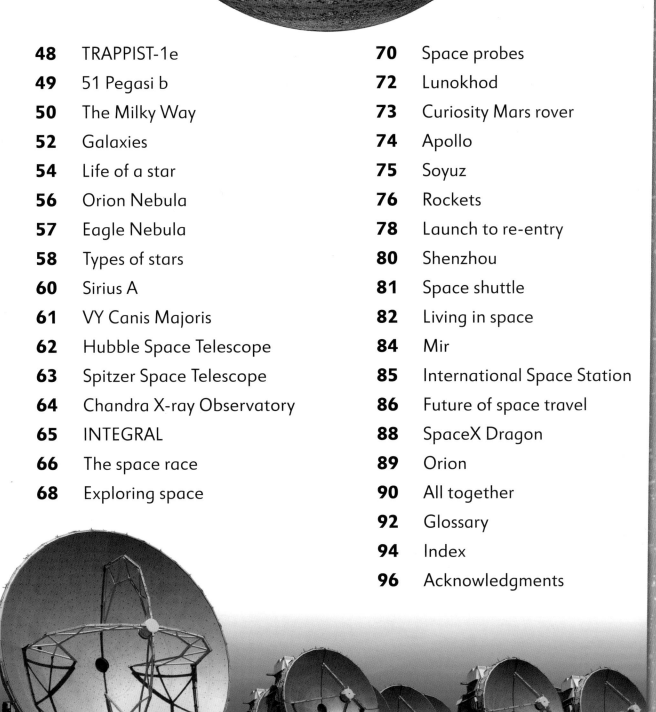

48	TRAPPIST-1e	70	Space probes
49	51 Pegasi b	72	Lunokhod
50	The Milky Way	73	Curiosity Mars rover
52	Galaxies	74	Apollo
54	Life of a star	75	Soyuz
56	Orion Nebula	76	Rockets
57	Eagle Nebula	78	Launch to re-entry
58	Types of stars	80	Shenzhou
60	Sirius A	81	Space shuttle
61	VY Canis Majoris	82	Living in space
62	Hubble Space Telescope	84	Mir
63	Spitzer Space Telescope	85	International Space Station
64	Chandra X-ray Observatory	86	Future of space travel
65	INTEGRAL	88	SpaceX Dragon
66	The space race	89	Orion
68	Exploring space	90	All together
		92	Glossary
		94	Index
		96	Acknowledgments

What is space?

The universe is everything around us—the planets, moons, billions of stars, and space. Space is what we call the enormous regions between astronomical objects. Space is almost completely empty, besides being thinly scattered with gas and dust.

What is gravity?

Gravity is an invisible force that pulls everything toward the center of an object. Objects with a higher mass have a stronger force of gravity. Earth's gravity keeps us on the ground, while the sun has so much gravity that planets orbit (travel around) it.

Why is space black?

During the day, planet Earth looks lit up. This is because the air in Earth's atmosphere scatters light from the sun in different directions. In space, there is hardly any air to scatter the sun's light, so it looks black.

Sunrise on Earth

Where does space begin?

Earth's atmosphere is made of layers of gases. It gets thinner and thinner the higher you go. Scientists imagine a boundary around 62 miles (100 km) above the Earth's surface called the Kármán line, which is where space begins. Satellites and space stations orbit the Earth beyond this line—and any person who crosses it is counted as an astronaut.

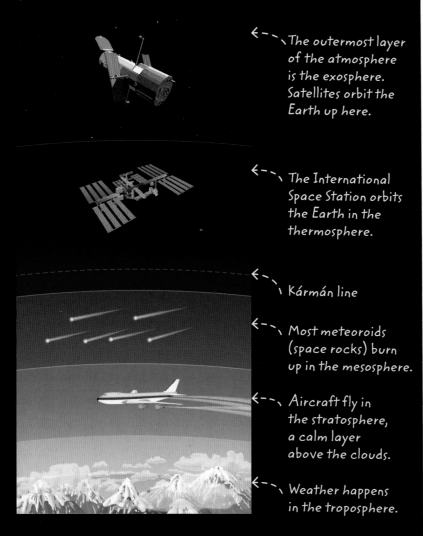

← The outermost layer of the atmosphere is the exosphere. Satellites orbit the Earth up here.

← The International Space Station orbits the Earth in the thermosphere.

← Kármán line

← Most meteoroids (space rocks) burn up in the mesosphere.

← Aircraft fly in the stratosphere, a calm layer above the clouds.

← Weather happens in the troposphere.

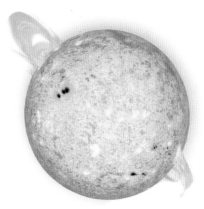

What is a star?

A star is a ball of hot gases, which are constantly burning to produce heat and light. Stars are held together by gravity. The closest star to Earth is the sun.

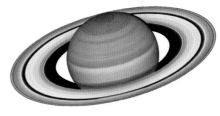

What is a planet?

Planets are large balls of rock or gas that orbit a star. Each planet has its own force of gravity, which pulls it into a spherical (round) shape.

Moon

What is a moon?

Any object that orbits a larger object in space is called a satellite. A moon is a natural satellite. Moons travel around planets and even some asteroids (chunks of rock or metal that orbit the sun).

5

Looking at the sky

If you look up at the sky on a clear night, you will see hundreds, if not thousands, of stars. Astronomy is the name given to the study of planets, stars, and other things in space. It helps us learn more about the universe and everything in it. People have been studying the night sky for centuries.

Early astronomers found patterns of stars in the sky, called constellations, and gave each its own name. These helped them tell stars apart.

Mapping the night sky

Ancient humans created maps of the night sky, known as star charts or sky charts. These charts helped them to find their way across land and sea, since they could figure out their direction based on the position of the constellations in the sky.

Ancient astronomy

Ancient humans studied the night sky just by using their eyes. They noted the movement of the sun, and the movement and changing phases of the moon. They figured out the length of a year on Earth, as well as the size of the planet.

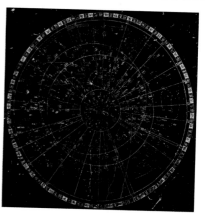

Star chart

Built in the Stone Age, this group of rocks, called Stonehenge, may have been created as a way to track the movement of the sun. It is located in Wiltshire in southern England.

Early ideas

Until the 16th century, many people believed that the Earth was at the center of the solar system. In 1543, Polish astronomer Nicolaus Copernicus disagreed with this, and correctly suggested that all of the planets in the solar system orbit, or move around, the sun.

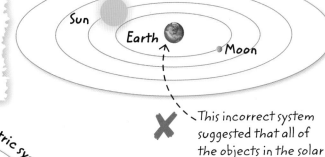

Geocentric system

This incorrect system suggested that all of the objects in the solar system orbit the Earth.

Heliocentric system

This system places the sun at the center of the solar system, and shows that all of the planets orbit around it.

The telescope

Invented in around 1609, this tool allows the user to see objects that are far away. It works by collecting light from an object, and making the image of the object bigger by using mirrors and curved pieces of glass called lenses.

Replica of Galileo's telescope

Italian astronomer and physicist Galileo Galilei built his own telescope. He was one of the first people to study the night sky using a telescope.

Modern astronomy

Modern astronomers use big telescopes that are located all over the world to look at the sky. Some of these telescopes are actually in space themselves! Astronomers often use computers to control them. The telescopes then send images of space back to the computer for astronomers to study.

This astronomer is working in the control room at the Mount Graham International Observatory in Arizona, USA.

Orion

Orion is one of the most well-known constellations in the night sky. It is named after a giant hunter in Greek mythology. The constellation contains the Orion Nebula, an area where new stars are forming.

Bellatrix is a massive star that forms the left shoulder of Orion, the hunter.

Betelgeuse is the second brightest star in the Orion constellation. It makes up the hunter's right shoulder.

The Orion constellation is easily recognized by the three bright stars that line up to form Orion's belt.

Global constellation

The Orion constellation can be seen from all around the world, although viewers in the Southern Hemisphere would see it upside down, with Orion's feet at the top. The easiest way to find Orion is to look for Orion's belt.

Rigel is the brightest star in the constellation. It represents the left foot of Orion, the hunter.

Orion's belt

The main stars of the Orion constellation visible in the night sky

There are 88 internationally recognized constellations in the night sky.

Ursa Major

Meaning "The Great Bear," Ursa Major is the third largest constellation in the night sky. It contains the well-known Big Dipper, or Plough, asterism (a pattern of stars within a constellation).

Fact file

» **Where to view:** Northern Hemisphere
» **Best viewed in:** May
» **Number of bright stars:** 7
» **Brightest star:** Alioth

Mizar and Alcor are a pair of stars that appear very close to each other from Earth. This is known as a double star system.

Also known as Epsilon Ursae Majoris, Alioth is the brightest star in the constellation.

Dubhe, and the star below it, called Merak, are known as pointer stars since they are used to locate Polaris, the North Star.

Ursa Major's seven bright stars form a saucepan shape known as the Big Dipper.

The North Star

Ursa Major can be used to find Polaris, the North Star, which sits almost directly above Earth's North Pole. Following a straight line up from the pointer stars takes you directly to Polaris, which is part of the Ursa Minor constellation.

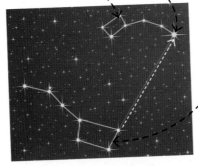

Ursa Minor · Polaris

Locating the North Star from Ursa Major

Ursa Major

The Ursa Minor constellation represents a small bear. Sometimes known as the Little Dipper, its stars form a smaller saucepan shape above Ursa Major.

9

Constellations

Most of the 88 constellations in the night sky can only be seen from some parts of the world at any time. This is because only half of the sky can be seen from any point on Earth—the planet itself covers the other half. Stars are often much farther apart than they look in the sky, because some are closer to Earth than others.

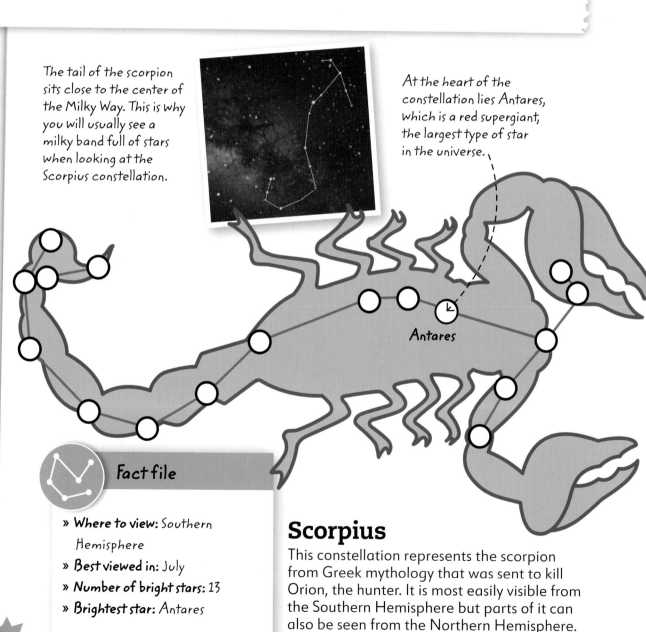

The tail of the scorpion sits close to the center of the Milky Way. This is why you will usually see a milky band full of stars when looking at the Scorpius constellation.

At the heart of the constellation lies Antares, which is a red supergiant, the largest type of star in the universe.

Antares

Fact file

» **Where to view:** Southern Hemisphere
» **Best viewed in:** July
» **Number of bright stars:** 13
» **Brightest star:** Antares

Scorpius

This constellation represents the scorpion from Greek mythology that was sent to kill Orion, the hunter. It is most easily visible from the Southern Hemisphere but parts of it can also be seen from the Northern Hemisphere.

Fact file

» **Where to view:** Northern Hemisphere
» **Best viewed in:** February
» **Number of bright stars:** 6
» **Brightest star:** Pollux

Gemini

Gemini is one of the oldest constellations, visible in the northern sky. Gemini means "twins" in Latin and represents two mythical twin brothers, Castor and Pollux. The two stars named after the brothers are the brightest in the constellation.

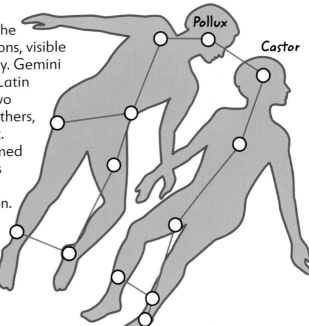

Pollux

Castor

THE SMALLEST CONSTELLATION

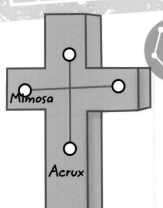

Mimosa

Acrux

Fact file

» **Where to view:** Southern Hemisphere
» **Best viewed in:** May
» **Number of bright stars:** 4
» **Brightest star:** Acrux

Crux

Despite being the smallest constellation, Crux is one of the most easy to see in the night sky, thanks to its recognizable shape. It is also known as the Southern Cross, and its stars have been used since ancient times to find the South Pole.

Fact file

» **Where to view:** Northern Hemisphere
» **Best viewed in:** November
» **Number of bright stars:** 5
» **Brightest star:** Alpha Cassiopeiae (Schedar)

Cassiopeia

The five bright stars in the Cassiopeia constellation form a "W"-shaped pattern, which makes it easy to spot in the night sky. The constellation is named after a mythical queen from ancient Greece.

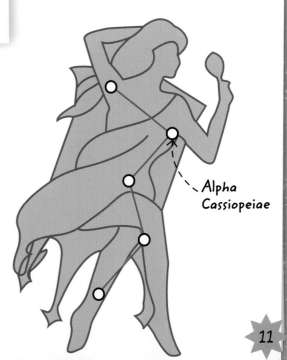

Alpha Cassiopeiae

Observatories

Observatories are places that house some of the largest telescopes. Most are located in unpopulated areas with good weather away from artificial light and pollution, such as on mountaintops and in deserts. This gives astronomers a much clearer view of the night sky.

Atacama Large Millimeter Array (ALMA)

ALMA is made up of sixty-six antennas that act together as a single giant radio telescope. Radio telescopes work by picking up radio waves from galaxies and stars in the universe. A receiver measures the waves as they come in. The information is then turned into a picture by a computer.

Fact file

» **Location:** Atacama Desert, Chile
» **Size of antenna:** 54 with a 39 ft (12 m) diameter and 12 with a 23 ft (7 m) diameter
» **Type of telescope:** Radio telescope
» **In use:** 2013—present

Each dish can be moved around to point at a specific part of the sky.

Fact file

» **Location:** California, USA
» **Size of lens:** 36 in (91 cm)
» **Type of telescope:**
   Refracting telescope
» **In use:** 1888–present

Lick Observatory

This was the first permanent mountaintop observatory. Its original telescope was a refractor, which is still in use today. Refracting telescopes use a glass lens to collect and focus light from objects in the night sky.

The telescope is housed in a large dome, which can be rotated to allow astronomers to study different parts of the sky. --

Fact file

» **Location:** Hawaii, USA
» **Size of mirror:**
   11.7 ft (3.5 m)
» **Type of telescope:**
   Reflecting telescope
» **In use:** 1979–present

The "Great Lick Refractor," as the telescope is known, was the largest refracting telescope in the world when it was first built.

Canada-France-Hawaii Telescope

This is one of twelve observatories located on the summit of Mauna Kea, a 13,780 ft (4,200 m) high mountain in Hawaii. It houses a reflecting telescope, which uses mirrors to collect the light from objects in space.

The telescope was installed in the Paris Observatory in the 1800s. A dome was built to house the telescope. --

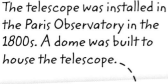

Fact file

» **Location:** Paris, France
» **Size of lens:**
   15 in (38 cm)
» **Type of telescope:**
   Refracting telescope
» **In use:** 1671–present

Paris Observatory

This is the world's oldest observatory to have continuously been in use since its creation. Many remarkable discoveries have been made here, including four of Saturn's moons in 1671–1684.

Our place in space

The universe is a very big place, so big in fact that it is hard to imagine everything that is in it. The Earth, the planets, the sun, and the things that you see in the night sky are just a few tiny objects that are part of the enormous universe.

Our solar system is part of a galaxy called the Milky Way. It is a spiral-shaped galaxy that contains between one hundred to four hundred billion stars.

The solar system is made up of a star called the sun, the eight planets that orbit around it, and other objects, such as dwarf planets, asteroids, and comets.

Our home, the planet Earth, is one of the eight planets in the solar system. Earth has all of the ingredients needed for life to exist, such as water, energy, oxygen, and soil.

What is a light year?

A light year is a unit of measurement—it represents the distance that light travels in one year. Light years are used to measure how far away objects in the universe are from each other. One light year is equal to roughly 5.9 trillion miles (9.5 trillion km).

It is estimated that there are at least two hundred billion galaxies in the universe. They come in all different shapes and sizes.

The Milky Way is one of the many galaxies that form part of the Local Group of galaxies. This group is made up of more than fifty different galaxies. The Local Group is roughly ten million light years across in size.

The Big Bang

Scientists believe that the universe started growing after a huge explosion, called the Big Bang, took place around 13.8 billion years ago. Before this happened, it is thought that nothing existed.

Illustration of what the Big Bang may have looked like

Earth

Alpha Centauri, the nearest star, is four light years away.

Canis Major, the nearest dwarf galaxy, is 3,700 light years away.

Andromeda, the nearest spiral galaxy, is 2.5 million light years away from Earth.

| 10 | 100 | 1,000 | 10,000 | 100,000 | 1 million | 10 million |

Distance in light years from Earth
(not to scale)

Solar system

The solar system is our home in space. In the center is a star, the sun. A collection of objects travels around the sun on paths called orbits. These include eight planets and their moons, five known dwarf planets, and countless asteroids, meteoroids, and comets.

Saturn

An orbit is a curved path that an object follows in space. Each of the eight planets follows its own orbit around the sun.

Earth

Mars

Venus

Mercury

The sun is a yellow dwarf star. It uses a pulling force called gravity to keep the objects in the solar system orbiting around it.

Asteroids are lumps of metal and rock that orbit the sun. Most of them are found in the asteroid belt between Mars and Jupiter.

Other planetary systems

Our sun is not the only star to have planets orbiting it. Scientists have discovered thousands of different systems with planets in our galaxy, the Milky Way. Some of these systems only have one planet, while others have many.

Kepler-16b is a planet that orbits not just one, but two stars!

Pluto

At the edge of the solar system is the Kuiper Belt. This ring is home to some of the dwarf planets and comets.

Neptune

Comets are objects made of dust and ice. When they get close to the sun, they heat up and some of their ice turns into a bright tail.

Jupiter

Uranus

Planet types

There are three types of planets in the solar system: rocky, gas giant, and ice giant. The rocky planets are the four closest to the sun. The gas and ice giants are the four planets farthest away from the sun.

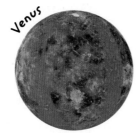
Venus

Rocky planets have a solid surface. The rocky planets are Mercury, Venus, Earth, and Mars.

Jupiter

Gas giants are mostly made of gas. The two gas giants are Jupiter and Saturn.

Neptune

Ice giants are mostly made of ice and gas. The two ice giants are Uranus and Neptune.

The sun

The sun is the only star in our solar system. The sun's gravity stops the planets from flying off into space. Its surface sends out a lot of heat, light, and other energy into space.

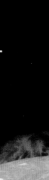

⚠️ Never look directly at the sun—it can damage your eyes!

Sunspots are dark areas that are cooler than the rest of the sun's surface.

A large loop of gas that shoots out from the sun's surface is called a solar prominence.

Solar flares are sudden explosions of energy on the sun's surface.

Solar power

Sunlight can be used to make electricity. This is called solar power. Solar panels take in energy from sunlight and turn it into electricity.

A house with solar panels on its roof

The sun makes up 99.8 percent of the entire mass of our solar system.

Inside the sun

The sun is a huge ball made up of hot gases, mostly hydrogen and helium. It has five layers. These are the solar atmosphere, photosphere, convective zone, radiative zone, and core.

» **Type of star:** Yellow dwarf
» **Size:** 864,000 miles (1.4 million km) in diameter
» **Age:** 4.5 billion years old
» **Surface temperature:** 10,000°F (5,500°C)

The fiery photosphere is often called the sun's surface.

In the convective zone, heat is transported by large bubbles of hot gas that move upward.

Energy from the core moves up through the radiative zone. It can take thousands of years for this energy to reach the surface.

The core is scorching hot—it reaches temperatures of 27 million°F (15 million°C).

The sun's atmosphere has two layers: the red-orange colored chromosphere, and the corona, which is a layer of gas that extends far into space.

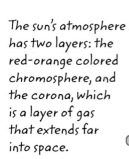

Pioneer 6

Pioneer 6 was one of the first spacecraft sent to study the sun. It was launched in 1965.

Auroras

At the Earth's poles, amazing displays of light, called auroras, can sometimes be seen. These occur when particles from the sun hit the Earth's atmosphere.

Mercury

Mercury is the closest planet to the sun, and the smallest. It is only slightly larger than our moon and looks very similar, being gray and heavily cratered. Mercury orbits the sun faster than any other planet.

Caloris Basin is one of the largest impact craters in the solar system. It is so big that the whole of the British Isles could fit inside it.

Bright streaks, called rays, are created when particles are blasted out from a crater during a collision.

Mercury's surface has many craters, which are the result of asteroids crashing into its surface.

Hot and cold

Mercury is so close to the sun that temperatures in the day can reach a scorching 800°F (430°C). However, they drop to a freezing -290°F (-180°C) at night, since the thin atmosphere cannot trap in the sun's heat.

Mercury, half lit up by the sun

Inside Mercury

Mercury is a rocky planet—it has a solid surface that you could walk on. Unlike most other planets, it has a large core, which is unusual for such a small planet. The mantle and crust are much thinner by comparison.

> » **Distance from sun:**
>   36 million miles
>   (58 million km)
> » **Length of day:**
>   176 Earth days
> » **Length of year:**
>   88 Earth days
> » **Surface temperature:**
>   -290–800°F (-180–430°C)
> » **Number of moons:** 0

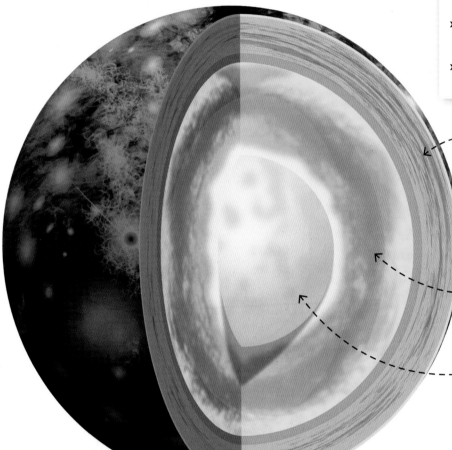

Mercury's mantle is made of rocky material and is much thinner than those of other planets in the solar system.

Mercury's outer core is liquid and made of metals, mostly iron.

The large inner core is solid. Together, the liquid and solid core make up around 85 percent of the planet.

Mercury has a thin crust that is full of hills and mountain ranges.

Exploring Mercury

The spacecraft MESSENGER observed Mercury from 2011 to 2015. It took photographs of almost the entire surface, and studied the planet's interior. MESSENGER was the first spacecraft to orbit Mercury.

MESSENGER orbiting Mercury

21

Venus

Named after the Roman goddess of love and beauty, Venus is the second planet from the sun. It is the second brightest object in our night sky, after the moon.

Like Earth, Venus has mountain ranges. Its highest peak is called Skadi Mons, in the Maxwell Montes mountain range.

Venus has many volcanoes, some of which are still active. Lava floods the surface of the planet when they erupt.

Venus is covered in thick, yellow clouds made of a harmful chemical called sulphuric acid.

Deadly planet

Seen from above, Venus looks peaceful with its pale clouds. However, the atmosphere is thick and poisonous, hiding a scorching, lifeless world beneath. Scientists believe Venus is a fiery orange color under the clouds.

Venus above and below the clouds

The solid surface of Venus is relatively smooth, unlike the craters found on the other rocky planets. This is due to the lava from erupting volcanoes.

Inside Venus

Venus is a rocky planet with a very thick atmosphere that permanently covers the planet. The structure of Venus is very similar to Earth. It has an iron core, along with a liquid mantle and a thin crust.

» **Distance from sun:**
67 million miles
(108 million km)
» **Length of day:**
243 Earth days
» **Length of year:**
225 Earth days
» **Surface temperature:**
880°F (471°C)
» **Number of moons:** 0

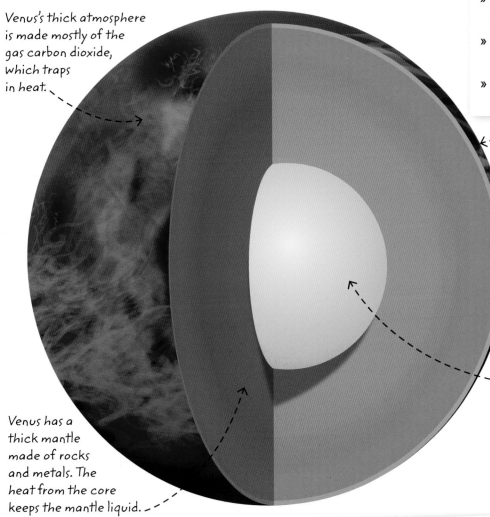

Venus's thick atmosphere is made mostly of the gas carbon dioxide, which traps in heat.

The thin crust is made of rocks. Volcanoes form on the surface when the crust moves as a result of the continually shifting mantle underneath.

Venus has a thick mantle made of rocks and metals. The heat from the core keeps the mantle liquid.

The outer part of Venus's large core is liquid, but it is solid in the center. The core is made of metal.

Earth's evil twin

Venus spins in the opposite direction to Earth but, being of a similar size and structure, is nicknamed "Earth's twin." However, the two planets have nothing else in common. The heat and poisonous gases on Venus mean humans would never survive there.

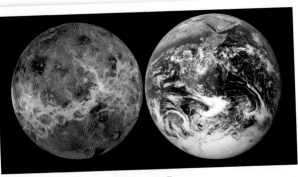

Venus and Earth

Earth

The third planet from the sun is our home, Earth. It is the only place in the universe that we currently know is home to living things. It is a rocky planet with a solid surface and liquid water.

Earth is the only planet in the solar system to have liquid water on its surface.

Thin ice floats in the sea of the Arctic at the top of the planet, while Antarctica at the bottom is a solid continent of large ice sheets.

Oceans cover nearly 70 percent of the surface. They hold 97 percent all of the water on Earth.

Earth's solid surface is made of rock. The land can take many forms, such as mountains, volcanoes, and valleys.

Made of tiny droplets of water, clouds help to control the temperature on Earth. They reflect heat away from the sun and trap in heat from the surface of Earth.

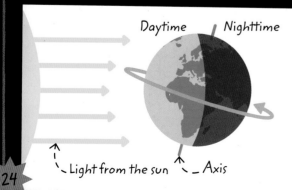

Daytime   Nighttime

Light from the sun   Axis

Day and night

Earth is always spinning on its axis—an imaginary line running through its center. As it spins, half of the planet faces the sun and experiences daytime, while the other half faces away from it and experiences nighttime.

Inside Earth

Earth is mainly made of rocky materials, as well as metals. The outer layer of the planet is called the crust. Under the crust are three more layers—the mantle, the outer core, and the inner core.

Fact file

» **Distance from sun:**
   93 million miles
   (150 million km)
» **Length of day:** 24 hours
» **Length of year:** 365 days
» **Surface temperature:**
   -128–136°F (-89–58°C)
» **Number of moons:** 1

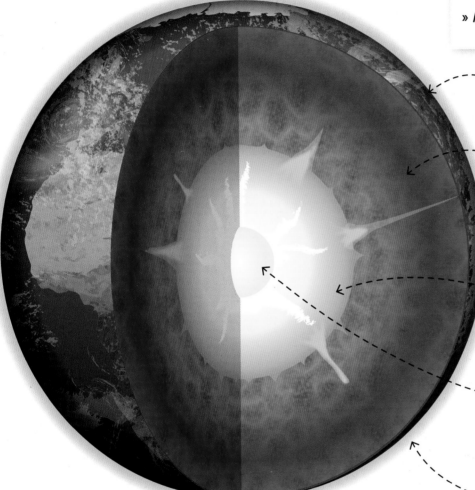

Earth's crust is made of soil and rock. The crust is thicker on land than on the ocean floor.

Under the crust is the mantle, which is Earth's thickest layer. It is made of very hot, thick liquid rock, called magma.

The outer core is made of liquid metals. It flows around the inner core.

Earth's metallic inner core is hot and solid. It is formed of iron and nickel.

A thick atmosphere surrounds Earth. It contains a mixture of gases, including oxygen, nitrogen, and carbon dioxide.

Safety bubble

Earth's atmosphere helps to protect us from space rocks and harmful rays from the sun. It breaks up smaller rocks into pieces, which then burn up before they can reach the planet's surface.

Atmosphere

The moon

The moon is an object that orbits planet Earth, and is bright enough to be easily seen in the night sky. It was likely formed billions of years ago when an asteroid crashed into Earth.

There is soil on the moon, but it is very different than soil on Earth. This soil is mainly made from powdered rock dust.

Astronauts first set foot on the moon in 1969. They landed in a smooth area called the Sea of Tranquility. Despite the name, it contains no water.

These dark areas of the surface are filled with solid lava. Early astronomers thought they might be seas.

The moon's surface is covered with craters. Tycho crater is one of the easiest craters to spot from Earth.

The heavily cratered areas of the moon's surface are called the Highlands.

Phases of the moon

The moon seems to change shape as it orbits the Earth. This is because the sun lights up different areas of it. These apparent changes are called phases.

 New moon

Waxing crescent

 First quarter

 Waxing gibbous

 Full moon

Waning gibbous

 Third quarter

 Waning crescent

The eight phases of the moon

Inside the moon

The moon is a very dry place with no air or water. It is made up of a core, a mantle, and a crust. The moon's rotation is locked to Earth, which means that the same side always faces Earth while the other side faces away.

Fact file

» **Distance from Earth:** 238,855 miles (384,400 km)
» **Orbital period:** 27 days
» **Size:** 2,159 miles (3,475 km) in diameter

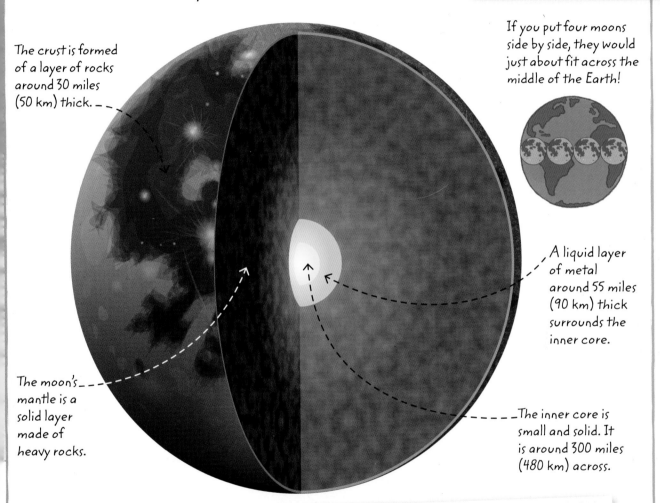

The crust is formed of a layer of rocks around 30 miles (50 km) thick.

If you put four moons side by side, they would just about fit across the middle of the Earth!

A liquid layer of metal around 55 miles (90 km) thick surrounds the inner core.

The moon's mantle is a solid layer made of heavy rocks.

The inner core is small and solid. It is around 300 miles (480 km) across.

Solar eclipse

A solar eclipse happens when the moon comes between Earth and the sun on its orbit around the planet. It blocks the sun's light, casting a shadow of darkness on Earth.

The moon covers the sun during a solar eclipse.

27

Mars

Half the size of Earth, Mars is known as the Red Planet because of the reddish dust covering its surface. Named after the Roman god of war, it is the fourth planet from the sun.

Olympus Mons is the largest volcano in the solar system.

Like Earth, Mars has ice caps at its poles. The north pole's ice caps melt in summer.

The northern hemisphere has a smooth surface. It is believed that there was once an ocean here.

Mars has many volcanoes, the largest of which is Olympus Mons. It is three times taller than Mount Everest.

The southern hemisphere is rough and has a large number of impact craters.

Valles Marineris is a huge canyon system that has formed a massive crack in the planet's surface. It is as long as the USA.

Irregular moons

Mars's moons, Phobos and Deimos, are thought to be asteroids captured by the planet's gravity when they were blasted in its direction during a collision with another object. Phobos is the larger moon, while Deimos is half its size.

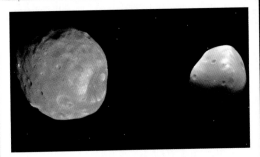

Martian moons, Phobos and Deimos

Inside Mars

Mars is a rocky planet that is cold and dry. It is surrounded by a very thin atmosphere, and like Earth, has seasons. The surface of Mars is covered in soil containing iron oxide, which is similar to rusty iron.

» **Distance from sun:**
  142 million miles
  (228 million km)
» **Length of day:** 24.6 hours
» **Length of year:** 687
  Earth days
» **Surface temperature:**
  -225–95°F (-143–35°C)
» **Number of moons:** 2

Mars's crust is a solid shell unlike Earth's crust, which is broken up into plates.

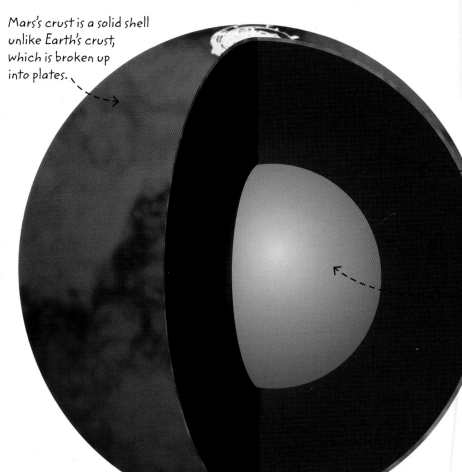

Between the core and crust lies Mars's mantle. The mantle is a thick layer of semi-liquid rock.

Mars has a small, solid core made of iron and other metals.

Dust storms

Winds on Mars create dust storms, which often last for weeks. Some are large enough to cover the entire planet, and the dust can take months to settle down after the storm has passed.

The size of a microwave, Sojourner was the first rover to land on another planet. It arrived on Mars in July 1997 and spent three months collecting information about the planet.

A "dust devil" on Mars

29

Jupiter

Named after the king of the Roman gods, Jupiter is the fifth planet from the sun, orbiting between the asteroid belt and Saturn. It is so big that it can be seen in the night sky without a telescope. Jupiter's rings are too faint to be seen from Earth.

Jupiter spins faster than any other planet in the solar system, causing powerful winds. These winds create bands of colorful clouds in the atmosphere.

The Great Red Spot is a giant storm that has been raging for hundreds of years.

Rings of dust

In 1979, the Voyager 1 probe discovered four very faint, reddish rings circling Jupiter. The rings are made of dust from meteorite impacts on Jupiter's moons, such as Adrastea and Metis.

Jupiter's main ring, as photographed by the Galileo spacecraft

Inside Jupiter

Jupiter is a gas giant planet—it does not have a solid surface. Just like the sun, Jupiter is made almost entirely of hydrogen and helium gas, but it is not big enough to be a star.

» **Distance from sun:**
484 million miles
(778 million km)
» **Length of day:** 9.9 hours
» **Length of year:** 11.8
Earth years
» **Surface temperature:**
-225 – -162°F
(-143 – -108°C)
» **Number of moons:** 79

Jupiter's thick clouds contain frozen ice crystals of ammonia, a chemical that smells like rotting fish.

Under the clouds is a liquid layer of hydrogen and helium. This is the largest ocean in the solar system.

Crushed under the pressure of the ocean above it, the liquid hydrogen in Jupiter's inner layer is metallic. This layer also contains helium.

Scientists think Jupiter's core could be solid or like an extremely hot, thick liquid. It is made of similar materials to those in Earth's core.

Galileo spacecraft

Launched in 1989, this probe spent eight years studying Jupiter's atmosphere and its largest moons.

Jupiter's moons

Jupiter has 79 known moons, including some of the biggest in the solar system. Most of Jupiter's moons are small, but the four largest ones are Ganymede, Europa, Callisto, and Io. They were discovered by Italian astronomer Galileo Galilei in the 17th century, and are known as the Galilean moons.

Europa has streaks and cracks. These are filled with minerals that have been frozen in ice.

A little less than half of Ganymede's surface is dark and rough. These areas are covered in craters.

Fact file

» **Distance from Jupiter:**
  665,115 miles (1,070,400 km)
» **Orbital period:** 7.2 days
» **Size:** 3,273 miles (5,268 km)
  in diameter

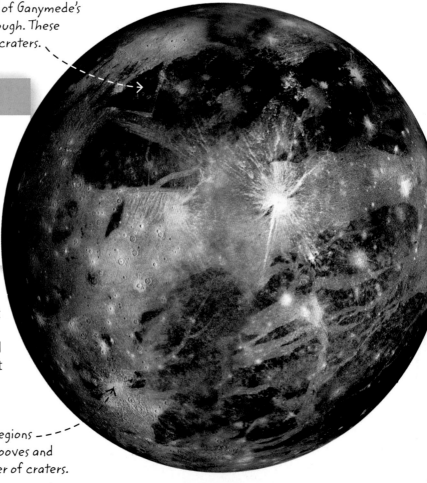

Ganymede

Ganymede is Jupiter's biggest moon. In fact, it is the largest moon in our solar system, and is even bigger than the planet Mercury. Ganymede is made of rock and water ice.

There are also light-colored regions on the surface. These have grooves and ridges, and only a small number of craters.

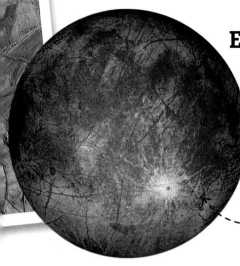

Europa

Europa is covered in a thin shell of water ice. It is thought that Europa is a great place to look for life because the sub-surface (just below the crust) may have water and the right mix of chemicals for life to exist.

Under the thin, icy shell of Europa's surface, scientists think there may be an ocean of liquid water or slushy ice.

Bright white spots on Callisto are thought to be peaks of the moon's craters that are covered with water ice.

Callisto

Covered in rocks and ice, Callisto has the oldest and the most heavily cratered surface of all Jupiter's moons. Most of these craters formed billions of years ago when meteorites crashed into Callisto's surface.

Eruptions from the moon's volcanoes can reach out far into space.

Io

This moon is the most volcanically active object in the solar system. Io's surface is covered in hundreds of volcanoes and lakes of molten lava. It has a yellow-orange color because there is a lot of the element sulphur on the surface.

Saturn

Known for its beautiful rings, Saturn is the sixth planet from the sun and the second largest in the solar system. It is the farthest planet that can be seen from Earth without a telescope.

Saturn has the highest number of moons in the solar system.

Winds at high speeds blow around the atmosphere, forming colorful clouds. The winds are caused by Saturn's fast rotation.

The gaps in Saturn's rings are created by moons that orbit the planet.

Saturn has seven main rings, which are made up of chunks of rock and ice.

Alphabet rings

The seven main rings are named alphabetically in the order they were discovered. "B" ring is the widest, and the brightest. It is twice as wide as Earth. Saturn's rings can be seen through a telescope.

B   A

False-color image of Saturn's rings

Inside Saturn

Like Jupiter, Saturn is mostly made of the gases hydrogen and helium. It has a small core that is surrounded by a liquid mantle. Above the mantle lies Saturn's atmosphere and its fainter cloud bands.

» **Distance from sun:** 886 million miles (1.4 billion km)
» **Length of day:** 10.7 hours
» **Length of year:** 29 Earth years
» **Surface temperature:** -218°F (-138°C)
» **Number of moons:** 82

Saturn's atmosphere has three main layers of clouds. The clouds form at different heights in the atmosphere so the layers are spread far apart.

The core is surrounded by a thick liquid layer of hydrogen.

Scientists think Saturn has a small, solid core. It is made of metals in the center, surrounded by rocky material.

Saturn is the least dense planet in the solar system. It is the only planet that could float on water!

Polar storm

Saturn's north pole is surrounded by a six-sided cloud pattern, which has a huge storm at the center. It was first seen by the Voyager 1 spacecraft in the early 1980s. Each side of the cloud is wider than Earth.

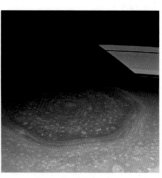

Saturn's hexagonal cloud pattern

35

Saturn's moons

Saturn has 82 known moons, the most of any planet in the solar system. Their sizes range from small boulders to huge objects bigger than Mercury. Some of Saturn's moons have unusual shapes—Atlas is a flat disc, while Pan looks a little like a flying saucer!

Turgis is the second largest known crater on Iapetus. It has steep slopes.

Fact file

» **Distance from Saturn:**
2,213,000 miles (3,561,000 km)
» **Orbital period:** 79.3 days
» **Size:** 914 miles (1,471 km)
in diameter

Iapetus

Discovered by Italian astronomer Giovanni Cassini in 1671, Iapetus is Saturn's third largest moon. It has a mountain range at its equator (middle) that is 6 miles (10 km) high. Iapetus is mostly made of water ice and some rocky material.

Fact file

» **Distance from Saturn:**
147,855 miles (237,948 km)
» **Orbital period:** 1.4 days
» **Size:** 313 miles (504 km)
in diameter

The surface of Enceladus is white, but this infrared image makes it appear blue.

Enceladus

Enceladus is Saturn's icy moon. Under a thin shell of ice, scientists think Enceladus may have a liquid ocean. NASA's Cassini spacecraft observed water shooting out of the ocean at Enceladus's south pole.

Hyperion

Hyperion is Saturn's largest non-spherical moon. Scientists think that Hyperion may have been formed from the debris of a larger moon that was destroyed in a collision. The surface is covered in deep craters, which give it a unique sponge-like look.

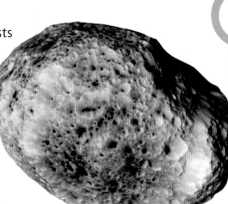

Titan

Titan is Saturn's largest moon. It is the second largest moon in the solar system, and the only one that has a thick atmosphere. Titan's atmosphere gives it an orange haze.

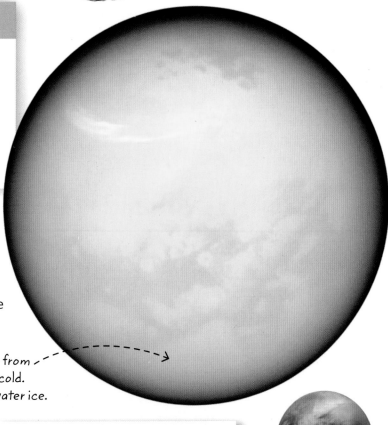

As Titan is so far away from the Sun, it is extremely cold. Its surface is made of water ice.

Shepherd moons

Some of Saturn's moons, such as Pan, orbit the planet between its rings. These are called shepherd moons as they "herd" ring particles around, moving them out of the way and keeping them contained within the rings.

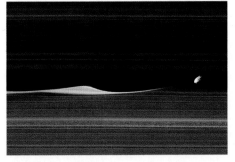

Pan's position between Saturn's rings

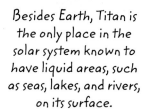

Besides Earth, Titan is the only place in the solar system known to have liquid areas, such as seas, lakes, and rivers, on its surface.

Uranus

Uranus is the seventh planet from the sun, and the third largest planet in the solar system. Uranus is the only planet in the solar system that is tilted on its side and spins sideways!

The poles take turns facing the sun. This means that seasons are very long—summers and winters at each pole last for twenty-one years!

Discovery of Uranus

Uranus was the first planet found using a telescope. William Herschel spotted it in 1781 from his garden in Bath, in the UK. He thought it was a comet or a star at first.

William Herschel

The methane gas in Uranus's atmosphere absorbs any red light from the sun. This makes the planet have a blue-green color.

Uranus has clouds that contain hydrogen sulphide. This is the gas that makes rotten eggs smell.

Uranus has thirteen rings. The outer rings have bright colors, while the narrower inner rings are dark in color.

Inside Uranus

Uranus is one of the coldest planets in the solar system and is known as an ice giant. Ice giants are made of a mix of icy materials and gas. Uranus is known for its blue-green color.

The thick atmosphere is made of hydrogen, helium, and methane gases.

A hot liquid mantle makes up most of the planet.

It is thought that Uranus may have a small core made of metals and rocks.

Scientists think that Uranus was hit and tipped over by an Earth-sized object as it was being formed!

Unusual moon

Miranda is one of Uranus's twenty-seven moons. It was discovered by Gerard Kuiper in 1948. Miranda's surface has strange features, including large cliffs and valleys that are deeper than the Grand Canyon!

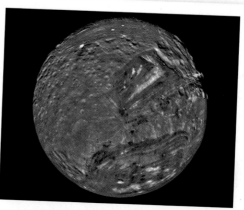

Miranda's rough surface

39

Neptune

In the solar system, Neptune is the farthest planet from the sun—around thirty times farther away than Earth. It is a dark, cold, and windy place. Neptune is named after the Roman god of the sea.

Bands of icy clouds are caused by fast-moving winds blowing around Neptune's atmosphere.

Storms are common on Neptune. In 1989, Voyager 2 noticed a giant storm called the Great Dark Spot.

Neptune has one of the fastest wind speeds in the solar system, up to 1,200 miles (2,000 km) per hour.

Voyager 2 visited Neptune in 1989.

Lone visitor

Voyager 2 is the only spacecraft to have visited Neptune. It flew past, coming as close as 3,076 miles (4,951 km) to the planet, before leaving the solar system. Voyager 2 studied Neptune's atmosphere and its moons Triton and Nereid.

Inside Neptune

Neptune is an ice giant, and the smallest of the four giant planets. Like the other giants, it is made mainly of hydrogen and helium. Similar to Uranus, Neptune has a small core, which is surrounded by an icy mantle and an atmosphere.

» **Distance from sun:**
   2.8 billion miles
   (4.5 billion km)
» **Length of day:**
   16 hours
» **Length of year:**
   165 Earth years
» **Surface temperature:**
   -331°F (-201°C)
» **Number of moons: 14**

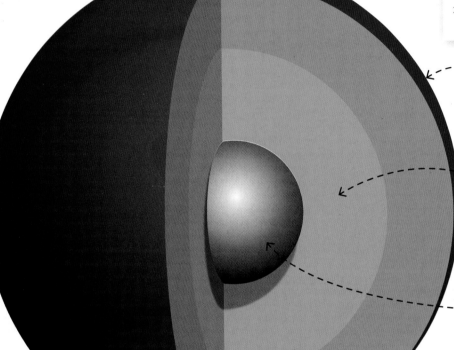

Neptune's thick atmosphere is made of the gases hydrogen, helium, and methane.

The mantle is a thick liquid made of icy materials. It contains water, methane, and other chemicals.

Scientists think Neptune has a small core at its center, made of metal and rock.

Triton is Neptune's largest moon. It has a smooth surface and a very thin atmosphere.

Hidden rings

Neptune has five main rings that are so faint they were only confirmed in 1989 when photographed by Voyager 2. The rings may be made of ice and dust. They are seen here lit up from behind by the sun.

Neptune's rings as seen from Voyager 2

Pluto

Pluto is a dwarf planet found in the outer solar system, beyond Neptune. Dwarf planets are smaller than planets and share their orbits around the sun with smaller objects made of rock and ice. Being so far from the sun, Pluto is a cold and icy world.

Much of Pluto's surface is covered in craters, mountains made of ice, and deep valleys.

Pluto has a very thin atmosphere made up of the gases nitrogen, methane, and carbon monoxide.

This crater-less, heart-shaped region is called Tombaugh Regio. It has smooth plains made of huge rivers of nitrogen ice.

Pluto's moons

Pluto's largest moon, Charon, is round and half its size. The other moons are much smaller and irregular in shape. All five moons are thought to have been formed from Pluto's collision with another object.

Styx

Nix

Kerberos

Hydra

Charon

Pluto's moons

Ceres

Found in the asteroid belt between Mars and Jupiter, Ceres is the largest asteroid in the solar system and is also classed as a dwarf planet. Made of rock and ice, Ceres makes up one-quarter of the material in the asteroid belt today.

NASA's Dawn spacecraft found bright spots on Ceres, shown here in enhanced color. These are places where salt from under the surface has collected.

The craters on Ceres are small and young. Any older craters were probably filled in by ice that may have erupted from volcanoes.

Ceres has a very thin atmosphere. Scientists have found water vapor that may have come from water ice on the surface.

The tallest mountain on Ceres, Ahuna Mons, is 3 miles (5 km) high.

LARGEST OBJECT IN THE ASTEROID BELT

The dwarf planet Makemake was discovered in the Kuiper Belt in 2005.

Discovery of Ceres

When it was first discovered, Ceres was thought to be a planet. It was renamed as an asteroid in the 1850s, after others were found in the asteroid belt. It was classed as a dwarf planet in 2006.

Italian astronomer Giuseppe Piazzi discovered Ceres in 1801.

Space rocks

As well as planets, moons, and the sun, there are many smaller objects in our solar system. Made of rock, ice, and metal, space rocks include asteroids, meteoroids, and comets. They are thought to be the pieces left over from when the planets formed, including rocks that failed to turn into planets.

A comet warms up as it gets closer to the sun. It then releases gases and dust that reflect sunlight.

Trojan asteroids share a planet's orbit around the sun. Jupiter has many trojan asteroids, in two groups.

The Kuiper Belt is a region of icy objects beyond Neptune's orbit. It includes comets and the dwarf planet Pluto.

Asteroids orbit the sun, and most are grouped in a large band between Mars and Jupiter called the asteroid belt.

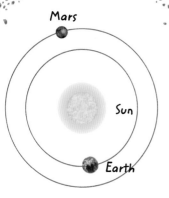

Mars

Sun

Earth

Jupiter

Asteroids

Most asteroids are irregularly shaped lumps of rock that orbit the sun. They are smaller than planets—many are the size of pebbles, but Ceres, the largest object in the asteroid belt, is 580 miles (930 km) in diameter. There are more than a million known asteroids in the solar system.

Comets

Often called dirty snowballs, comets are huge chunks of ice, dust, and rock that orbit the sun. A comet can be as big as a small town. There are currently more than 3,700 known comets.

The ball-shaped Oort Cloud is a collection of comets and other icy objects surrounding our entire solar system. It is the most distant region of our solar system.

Most comets are found in the Oort Cloud. A comet's orbit is shaped like a long oval.

A comet's nucleus (center) is made of ice and dust. Closer to the sun, the dust forms an expanding cloud called a coma.

Halley's Comet

The sun's wind blows dust off the comet, creating a separate dust tail.

As the comet warms up, the ice turns to gas and creates a gas tail behind the nucleus.

Meteoroids and meteorites

When an asteroid or a meteoroid enters Earth's atmosphere, its surface melts. This creates a flash of light called a meteor, or fireball. Sometimes, a piece of the rock remains and falls to the ground—it is then called a meteorite.

Meteoroid

Small chunks of rock or metal that travel through our solar system are called meteoroids.

ATMOSPHERE

SPACE

Meteor

A meteor, the bright streak of light we see in the night sky, is the hot air around a meteoroid as it slows down in the atmosphere.

Meteorites are space rocks that land on Earth. They have a thin, shiny, once-molten surface called "fusion crust."

Meteorite

EARTH

Vesta

Vesta is the second largest object in the asteroid belt, after Ceres. Unlike other asteroids, Vesta is big enough to have a crust, a mantle, and a core. It has two giant impact craters on its surface— Rheasilvia and Veneneia.

» **Distance from sun:** 223 million miles (359 million km)
» **Orbital period:** 3.6 years
» **Size:** 330 miles (531 km) in diameter
» **Discovery date:** 1807

BRIGHTEST ASTEROID IN THE NIGHT SKY

The surface is covered in dark material that was probably left over when other asteroids collided with Vesta.

Vesta's largest crater, Rheasilvia, is almost as wide as the asteroid itself, at 311 miles (500 km) across. It covers 95 percent of Vesta's surface.

Narrow channels in the ground, called troughs, circle the asteroid at its equator.

Asteroid orbiter

Reaching Vesta in 2011, Dawn became the first spacecraft to orbit an asteroid. It went on to explore Ceres, taking two and a half years to reach the dwarf planet.

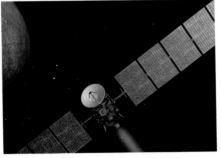

NASA's Dawn spacecraft

The Dawn mission confirmed that these meteorites found on Earth fell from Vesta.

Comet 67P/C-G

Comet 67P/Churyumov-Gerasimenko orbits the sun between Jupiter and Earth, but it was previously thought to have spent time orbiting in the Kuiper Belt at the edge of the solar system. It is the first comet to have had a spacecraft orbit and land on it.

Fact file

» **Distance from sun:** 115–528 million miles (186–850 million km)
» **Orbital period:** 6.4 years
» **Size:** 2.5 miles (4 km) long
» **Discovery date:** 1969

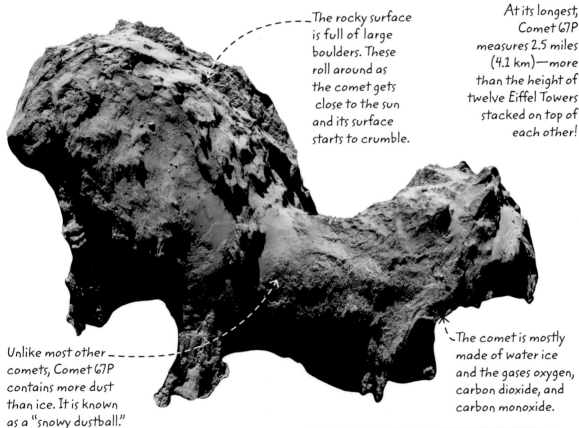

The rocky surface is full of large boulders. These roll around as the comet gets close to the sun and its surface starts to crumble.

At its longest, Comet 67P measures 2.5 miles (4.1 km)—more than the height of twelve Eiffel Towers stacked on top of each other!

Unlike most other comets, Comet 67P contains more dust than ice. It is known as a "snowy dustball."

The comet is mostly made of water ice and the gases oxygen, carbon dioxide, and carbon monoxide.

Comet landing

In 2014, after a journey of ten years, the spacecraft Rosetta reached Comet 67P. It dropped a dishwasher-sized probe called Philae onto the comet's surface. Philae spent two days carrying out scientific experiments and sent the information it collected back to Earth.

Philae on Comet 67P

TRAPPIST-1e

TRAPPIST-1e is an exoplanet orbiting a small, dim red star that is much cooler than our sun. Exoplanets are planets that have been discovered outside our solar system. Most exoplanets orbit a star.

TRAPPIST-1e is a terrestrial exoplanet, which means it is similar to Earth in its size, temperature, and gravity.

As it is a similar size to Earth, scientists believe the planet is made of rock or iron, with either a solid or a liquid surface.

It is thought that the Earth-like temperature on TRAPPIST-1e means there could be liquid water on its surface.

Goldilocks zone

Scientists can figure out how warm a planet is by measuring the distance at which it orbits its star, and the heat coming off the star. Liquid water exists between 32°F (0°C) and 212°F (100°C). If the temperature of a planet is within this range, it is said to be in the "Goldilocks zone" because it is not too hot or too cold, but just right. Three of the planets in the TRAPPIST-1 system are in the Goldilocks zone.

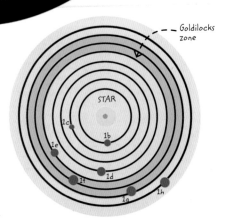

TRAPPIST-1 system

51 Pegasi b

51 Pegasi b was the first exoplanet to be discovered orbiting a sun-like star. It is known as a "hot Jupiter" because it is a huge planet and orbits very close to its star. The surface temperature is around 1,800°F (1,000°C).

» **Distance from Earth:** 50 light years
» **Length of year:** 4.2 Earth days
» **Size:** 168,801 miles (271,660 km) in diameter
» **Discovery date:** 1995

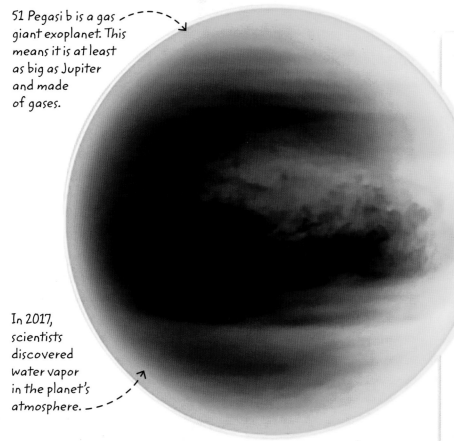

51 Pegasi b is a gas giant exoplanet. This means it is at least as big as Jupiter and made of gases.

In 2017, scientists discovered water vapor in the planet's atmosphere.

Kepler space telescope

Finding exoplanets

Launched in 2009, the Kepler space telescope spent nine years looking for planets outside our solar system. It found 2,662 of them, some of which may have the right conditions for life to exist!

Terrestrial Super-Earth Neptunian

As well as gas giants, exoplanets can be classed as terrestrial (rocky planets similar to Earth), Super-Earth (rocky planets much larger than Earth), or Neptunian (similar to Neptune).

Mercury is the nearest planet to the sun, but 51 Pegasi b is eight times closer to its star than Mercury is to our sun.

The Milky Way

Our solar system is part of a galaxy—an enormous collection of stars, planetary systems, gas, and dust—called the Milky Way. This galaxy is spiral shaped, with curved arms. Stars travel in and out of the arms as they make their way around the Milky Way.

The Scutum-Centaurus arm is one of the main spiral arms of the Milky Way. It contains both old and young stars.

The spiral arms contain a lot of gas and dust, the key ingredients that make up a star. This means they are ideal places for new stars to form.

A massive black hole lies at the center of the galaxy. Black holes are invisible because their gravity is so strong that not even light can escape.

The sun takes 230 million years to travel around the Milky Way.

Our solar system lies in the Orion arm, about one-third of the way out from the galaxy's center. Most of the stars we see in our night sky are in this arm.

The Perseus arm is another main arm of the Milky Way. This arm is closest to the Orion arm, where our sun is located.

Observing the Milky Way

It is possible to see the Milky Way from anywhere in the world. It is visible as a thick band of stars that divides the sky into two equal hemispheres. However, the stars are very faint, so the galaxy is best seen when there is no moonlight and very little artificial light pollution.

The view of the Milky Way is most spectacular from the southern half of Earth, as seen here at the La Silla Observatory in Chile.

The center of our galaxy is packed with old stars and huge dust clouds. The white area visible in this infrared and X-ray image is the Milky Way's galactic center.

Galaxies

A galaxy is a huge collection of stars, gas, and dust held together by the force of gravity. There are more than 100 billion stars in a typical galaxy and they come in four main shapes—spiral, elliptical, irregular, and lenticular.

Scientists think there are more than 100 billion galaxies.

Fact file

» **Type of galaxy:** Spiral
» **Distance from Earth:** 21 million light years
» **Size:** 170,000 light years across
» **Constellation:** Ursa Major

Pinwheel Galaxy

Often called M101, the Pinwheel Galaxy is a spiral galaxy that contains more than one trillion stars. It is almost twice the size of our enormous galaxy, the Milky Way.

The spiral galaxy Andromeda is our nearest major galaxy. It is moving toward our galaxy, the Milky Way. In around four billion years, the pair will pass through each other.

Spiral arms are regions of newborn stars that wind out from the galaxy's center.

- » **Type of galaxy:** Lenticular
- » **Distance from Earth:**
  44 million light years
- » **Size:** 60,000 light years
  across
- » **Constellation:** Draco

NGC 5866

Also called M102 or Spindle Galaxy, NGC 5866 is a lenticular galaxy—a galaxy with a central bulge of stars but no spiral arms. Lenticular galaxies have very few new stars forming in them.

A huge black hole at the center of M87 causes a jet of material to shoot out from the galaxy's core.

From Earth, we see the bright disc of NGC 5866 on its side.

M87

Elliptical galaxies are usually shaped like a ball or an egg. M87 is a giant elliptical galaxy with several trillion stars and a huge black hole at its center. It is the biggest galaxy in our region of the universe.

Fact file

- » **Type of galaxy:** Elliptical
- » **Distance from Earth:**
  54 million light years
- » **Size:** 120,000 light years
  across
- » **Constellation:** Virgo

Irregular galaxies are full of gas and dust and do not have a particular shape.

Fact file

- » **Type of galaxy:** Irregular
- » **Distance from Earth:**
  200,000 light years
- » **Size:** 7,000 light years
  across
- » **Constellation:**
  Tucana and Hydrus

Small Magellanic Cloud

This is one of two irregular dwarf galaxies orbiting our home galaxy, the Milky Way. Both the Small and Large Magellanic Cloud galaxies contain only a few hundred million stars.

Life of a star

Like humans, stars are born and eventually die. They are made mostly of hydrogen and helium gas, which is used to make heat and light. The mass of a star is the amount of material inside it. Low-mass stars can live for billions of years, while high-mass stars have a much shorter life.

Low-mass

High-mass

Yellow star

A star spends most of its life in what is known as the main sequence phase, burning hydrogen in its core. Our sun is currently in the yellow main sequence phase.

Blue star

The more massive a star is, the hotter it is and the quicker it uses up hydrogen. Blue stars are the hottest stars in the universe.

Red supergiant

When a high-mass star runs out of hydrogen, it becomes cooler, bigger, and redder. This type of star is called a supergiant, the biggest of all the stars.

Nebula

A nebula is a giant cloud of gas and dust inside which new stars are born. Gravity pulls the gas and dust together to form clumps. These clumps eventually collapse and heat up, forming stars.

Red giant

The star begins to get bigger and cool down as it starts to run out of hydrogen and nears the end of its life. It changes color and becomes known as a red giant.

Planetary nebula

Winds from the dying star push the outer layers away, which are shed to form an expanding shell of gas and dust around the core. This is called a planetary nebula.

White dwarf

The shell continues to expand into space until all that is left is a tiny, hot object called a white dwarf. It continues to cool over time, becoming dimmer and dimmer.

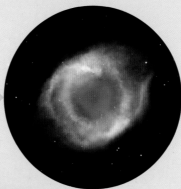

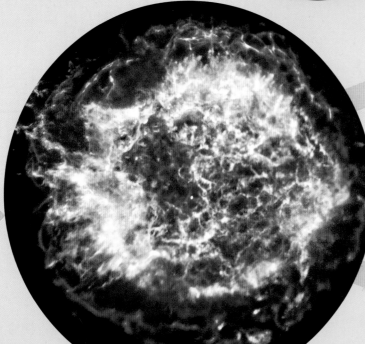

Neutron star

A supernova can leave behind a neutron star. The material from the exploded star shrinks down to as small as 12 miles (20 km) wide.

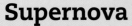

Supernova

The supergiant suddenly collapses, causing an explosion called a supernova. This is the largest kind of explosion in the universe and brighter than billions of suns!

Stellar black hole

For the most massive stars, the supernova leaves behind a black hole. This is a place in space where the pull of gravity is so strong that nothing can get out, not even light.

Orion Nebula

A nebula is a giant cloud of dust and gas in space. It is a region (area) where new stars are born. The Orion Nebula is one of the brightest nebulas, and it can be seen from Earth as a faint spot.

Fact file

» **Distance from Earth:** 1,340 light years
» **Location:** Orion constellation
» **Discovery date:** 1610

When strong winds from the new stars come together, they make a wave shape called a bow shock.

The nebula is lit up by bright young stars. Some of these stars are only a million years old.

Clouds of hydrogen gas in the nebula are lit up by nearby stars. This makes the nebula look red.

NEAREST STAR-FORMING REGION TO EARTH

Newborn stars

Many newly formed stars have a ring of gas and dust around them called a protoplanetary disc. The gas and dust eventually clump together to form new planets, moons, or asteroid belts.

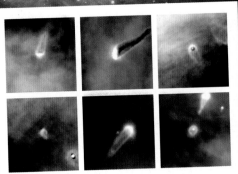

Protoplanetary discs in the Orion Nebula

Eagle Nebula

Also known as M16, the Eagle Nebula is an active star-forming region—a place where many new stars are being made. It is 5.5 million years old and can be seen from Earth with a small telescope.

» **Distance from Earth:** 7,000 light years
» **Location:** Serpens constellation
» **Discovery date:** 1745

The brighter regions in the Eagle Nebula are dense pockets of hotter gas, which have the potential to collapse into stars.

Dark clouds of dust block our view of stars forming inside the nebula.

There are over 8,000 young stars in the nebula, no more than 2–3 million years old.

Pillars of Creation

Pillars of Creation

These three towers of gas and dust found inside the Eagle Nebula were first discovered in 1995 by the Hubble Space Telescope. They are around five light years long, and many new stars are born inside them.

Types of stars

All stars may look the same to us but, depending on their age and mass, they differ by size, temperature, color, and luminosity (the amount of light they produce). Scientists sort stars into groups by comparing their luminosity to their temperature.

Brown dwarfs

Stars must be a certain size to burn hydrogen in the core. Brown dwarfs, also known as failed stars, begin as stars but do not get big enough to start burning hydrogen. They end up looking more like the planet Jupiter.

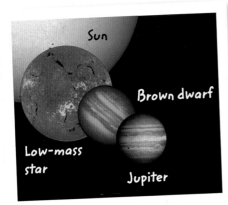

Brown dwarfs are bigger than Jupiter but smaller than low-mass stars.

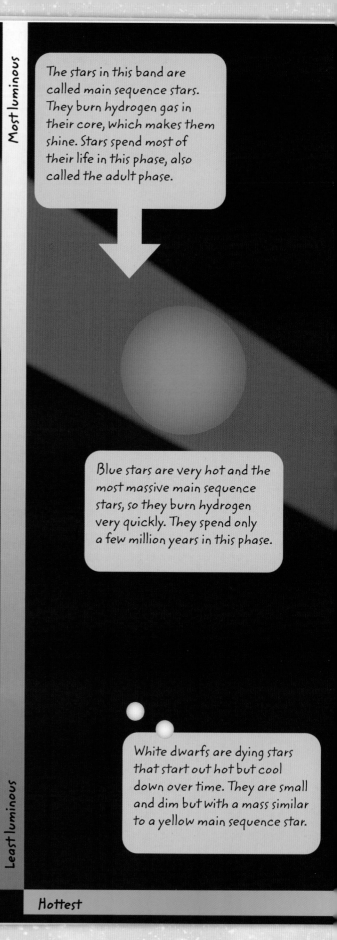

Most luminous

The stars in this band are called main sequence stars. They burn hydrogen gas in their core, which makes them shine. Stars spend most of their life in this phase, also called the adult phase.

Blue stars are very hot and the most massive main sequence stars, so they burn hydrogen very quickly. They spend only a few million years in this phase.

White dwarfs are dying stars that start out hot but cool down over time. They are small and dim but with a mass similar to a yellow main sequence star.

Least luminous

Hottest

The largest type of star, red supergiants are bright and cool. They only last up to a million years before exploding as a supernova.

Red giants are stars running out of hydrogen to burn and nearing the end of their life. They last for only a few hundred million years.

The sun is a yellow dwarf star. Yellow dwarfs stay in the main sequence phase for ten billion years. The sun is about halfway through its life.

Red dwarfs are the least massive and coolest main sequence stars. They burn hydrogen slowly, and live for hundreds of billions of years.

Sirius A

Named after the Greek word for "glowing," Sirius A is part of a binary star system (two stars that orbit each other). It is one of the closest stars to the sun and is almost twice as massive.

» **Distance from Earth:**
   8.6 light years
» **Type of star:**
   Blue main sequence
» **Age:** 230 million years
» **Constellation:** Canis Major

BRIGHTEST STAR IN THE NIGHT SKY

Sirius A is 450 times brighter than Sirius B. It is known as the primary star.

Discovery of Sirius B

On January 31, 1862, American telescope-maker and astronomer Alvan Clark first saw Sirius B—a dim star almost lost in the glow of Sirius A. He was testing a new telescope when he made the discovery.

Sirius A and B

Sirius B is a white dwarf star, tiny and faint. It is smaller than planet Earth.

Sirius star system

Sirius A is sometimes called the "Dog Star" because it is part of the Canis Major constellation, which looks like a large dog.

VY Canis Majoris

On average, around 1,800 times bigger than the sun, VY Canis Majoris is a red supergiant. It is a variable star, which means its brightness changes as seen from Earth. The star pulsates (gets bigger and smaller) over the course of 956 days.

Fact file

» **Distance from Earth:** 5,000 light years
» **Type of star:** Red supergiant
» **Age:** 8.2 million years
» **Constellation:** Canis Major

ONE OF THE LARGEST KNOWN STARS IN THE UNIVERSE

All around the star there are large grains of dust, which reflect starlight.

VY Canis Majoris has 30 to 40 times the mass of the sun and is 200,000 times more luminous.

As it pulsates, VY Canis Majoris loses material such as gas and dust. This forms dust shells, which look like rings of light around the star.

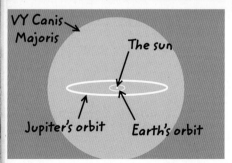

VY Canis Majoris is wider than Jupiter's orbit around the sun!

Dying giant

VY Canis Majoris is around 1,800 times bigger than the sun. Its huge size means it has weak surface gravity and loses mass easily. The star has already lost half of its total mass and will soon collapse to become a black hole.

Hubble Space Telescope

Orbiting the Earth, Hubble is one of the largest telescopes in space. It can detect ultraviolet, visible, and near-infrared light. Hubble has captured images of some of the most distant stars and galaxies yet found.

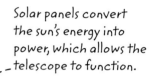
The antenna receives instructions and sends information in the form of radio waves.

Solar panels convert the sun's energy into power, which allows the telescope to function.

Images are captured through a hole called an aperture. A door shuts if the sun's light is bright enough to cause damage.

Repairing Hubble

Hubble is the only telescope that has been repaired in space. Astronauts have been sent up to fix it five times during its lifetime, and almost every part has been replaced.

An astronaut making repairs

Hubble Space Telescope is around the size of a school bus.

Spitzer Space Telescope

Spitzer was used to detect infrared light, which is invisible to our eyes. It was able to observe cooler objects such as brown dwarf stars, exoplanets, and dust in star-forming regions. The telescope weighs less than 110 lb (50 kg).

- » **Launch date:**
  August 2003
- » **Type of telescope:**
  Infrared
- » **Size of main mirror:**
  2.8 ft (0.85 m) in diameter
- » **Mission status:**
  Ended in 2020

The telescope's solar panels have a total of 784 solar cells.

The flying observatory

The Stratospheric Observatory for Infrared Astronomy (SOFIA) is a Boeing 747SP aircraft carrying an 8 ft (2.5 m) infrared telescope. It operates at night from a height of around 26,000 miles (42,000 km). Each flight lasts around ten hours.

SOFIA telescope

A tank of liquid helium kept the telescope cool for more than five years before running out.

A star tracker device points the telescope to the desired area of the sky without help from astronomers on Earth.

63

Chandra X-ray Observatory

This huge telescope studies X-rays, which are invisible light rays, produced by very hot regions in the universe. It is named after Subrahmanyan Chandrasekhar, a twentieth-century Indian-American astrophysicist.

To avoid damage from light, the sunshade door stays closed until Chandra is ready to take a picture.

Solar panels provide power, which is stored in three batteries.

The camera takes X-ray pictures of hot regions, such as supernovas.

Two thrusters keep Chandra orbiting at a steady height above the Earth.

THE WORLD'S MOST POWERFUL X-RAY TELESCOPE

Chandra is so efficient that it uses as little energy as a blow-dryer!

X-rays on Earth

X-rays are invisible waves of energy. They can pass through soft substances, such as skin, but not hard materials, such as metal or bone. Doctors use X-rays to take pictures of bones.

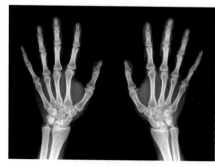

X-ray of hands

INTEGRAL

The International Gamma-Ray Astrophysics Laboratory (INTEGRAL) tracks the most energetic objects in space, such as supernova explosions and active galaxies. It detects gamma rays—the most powerful form of light.

The cameras and other scientific equipment are stored in an area called the payload module.

In addition to gamma rays, the imager can observe powerful X-rays from objects in space.

The service module stores equipment used to operate the fuel tanks, solar panels, and batteries.

Two solar panels generate power for the observatory. Each panel is 52.5 ft (16 m) long.

Balloon telescopes

Telescopes flown at heights of around 11–35 miles (18–57 km) can pick up microwaves, which are absorbed lower down in the atmosphere. Balloons are much cheaper than space telescopes.

Launched by India's space program in 2015, AstroSat orbits the Earth every ninety-eight minutes. It observes ultraviolet and X-rays from objects in space.

Balloon telescope

65

Laika
the dog

Luna 2

Yuri
Gagarin

Sputnik 1

Animal
in space

A stray dog named
Laika was the first
living thing to orbit
the Earth, on the
spacecraft Sputnik 2.

Spacecraft
landing

Luna 2 landed on
the moon, becoming
the first spacecraft to
land on another
object in space.

Human
in space

Cosmonaut (Russian
astronaut) Yuri Gagarin
was the first human in
space. He made one orbit
of Earth in Vostok 1.

First satellite

The Soviet Union
launched the first
artificial satellite,
Sputnik 1, to successfully
orbit Earth.

**November 3,
1957**

**September 12,
1959**

April 12, 1961

**October 4,
1957**

May 5, 1961

Explorer 1

**January 31,
1958**

American satellite

Explorer 1, the USA's first
artificial satellite in space, was
also the first satellite to carry
a scientific instrument.

American
in space

Alan Shepard Jr. was
the first US astronaut
to go to space, in the
Freedom 7 spacecraft.

The space race

Throughout the late 1950s and 1960s,
the USA and the Soviet Union (now Russia)
competed against each other to show which
country was better at space exploration. Each
of them wanted to be the first to achieve
important milestones in space.

Alan Shepard Jr.

Valentina Tereshkova

Alexei Leonov

Working together

Today, the USA and Russia often work together on space projects. In 2000, astronaut Bill Shepherd and cosmonauts Yuri Gidzenko and Sergei Krikalev completed Expedition 1, the first long-duration stay on the International Space Station.

The crew of Expedition 1 spent 136 days living aboard the ISS.

Woman in space

Cosmonaut Valentina Tereshkova became a national hero after she went to space in the Vostok 6 spacecraft.

First space walk

Attached to his craft by a rope, cosmonaut Alexei Leonov floated in space for ten minutes wearing a space suit.

June 16, 1963

March 18, 1965

Apollo 8 returns to Earth.

June 3, 1965

Ed White

December 21, 1968

July 20, 1969

Moon orbit

The USA's Apollo 8 crew became the first humans to successfully orbit another object in space—the moon.

Moon landing

Astronauts Neil Armstrong and Buzz Aldrin were the first humans to set foot on the moon as part of America's Apollo 11 mission.

American space walk

Astronaut Ed White spent twenty-three minutes outside his spacecraft during the Gemini 4 mission.

July 15, 1965

Mission to Mars

The USA's Mariner 4 mission flew by Mars, taking the first close-up pictures of the Red Planet.

Mariner 4

Neil Armstrong steps onto the moon.

NASA

US space agency NASA is leading the effort to send humans back to the moon under the Artemis program. Astronauts will be using new space suits with better flexibility for the mission.

James Webb Space Telescope

ESA

The European Space Agency (ESA) has twenty-two member states, and its headquarters are in Paris, France. The James Webb Space Telescope launches from Guiana Space Centre, the ESO's launch site.

Space suit engineer Kristine Davis

Cape Canaveral Air Force Station
Delivers cargo (supplies) to space stations

Vandenberg Air Force Base
Launches by NASA and private companies

Guiana Space Centre
Launches by ESA and private companies

Exploring space

Alcântara Launch Center
Satellite launches by the Brazilian Space Agency (AEB)

Many countries around the world are building new spacecraft, satellites, and tools to explore space. Government agencies and private companies are working on future space programs.

Launch site

Roscosmos

Based in Moscow, Roscosmos runs Russia's space activities. The mission control center in Korolyov guides all of the ongoing missions.

US mission patches

For every NASA mission, the crew members design a mission patch. The patches include the astronauts' names and mission number, as well as a picture to represent their work on the mission.

Apollo 11

STS-107

Baikonur Cosmodrome
Roscosmos's crewed and cargo launch facility

Jiuquan Satellite Launch Center
CNSA's launch site for human spaceflights

CNSA

China's space agency is currently working on building Tiangong, a modular space station, similar to Mir and the ISS.

Tanegashima Space Center
Japan's largest facility for launching rockets

Palmachim Airbase
Satellite launch site for the Israel Space Agency

Satish Dhawan Space Centre
ISRO's launch site for satellites and spaceflights to travel to other objects in the solar system

Artist's impression of Tiangong space station

Polar Satellite Launch Vehicle

ISRO

The Indian Space Research Organisation (ISRO) has many different launch vehicles—rockets that send spacecraft into space. ISRO launched India's first mission to the moon and to orbit Mars.

Space probes

Since the 1950s, humans have been sending spacecrafts called space probes to explore objects in our solar system. Space probes can orbit or even land on objects in space, and they contain tools that help scientists learn more about the universe.

In 2012, Voyager 1 became the first space probe to leave our solar system.

Cassini-Huygens

For more than thirteen years, the space probe Cassini studied Saturn, its rings, and its moons. It carried another space probe, called Huygens, which landed on Saturn's largest moon, Titan, in 2005.

Fact file

» **Launch date:** October 1997
» **Type of spacecraft:** Orbiter and Lander
» **Size:** 22.3 ft (6.8 m) long
» **Mission status:** Ended in 2017

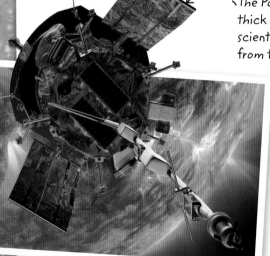

The Parker Solar Probe's thick shield protects the scientific instruments from the sun's heat.

Parker Solar Probe

Studying the sun, this probe has come to within 3.8 million miles (6.1 million km) of the star's surface, flying through the solar corona. It faces temperatures as high as 2,500°F (1,377°C).

Fact file

» **Launch date:** August 2018
» **Type of spacecraft:** Orbiter
» **Size:** 7.5 ft (2.3 m) long
» **Mission status:** Ongoing

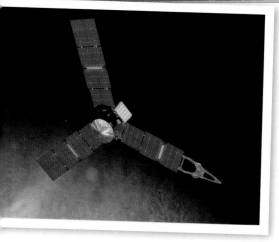

Juno

Launched to explore Jupiter, this space probe has orbited the planet above its north and south poles, studying its magnetic field. Juno can fly within 2,600 miles (4,200 km) of the top of Jupiter's clouds.

Fact file

» **Launch date:**
August 2011
» **Type of spacecraft:**
Orbiter
» **Size:** 11.5 ft (3.5 m) long
» **Mission status:** Ongoing

New Horizons

This was the first space probe to fly past dwarf planet Pluto, taking pictures of its surface and its moon, Charon. New Horizons went on to study a small Kuiper Belt object, now called Arrokoth.

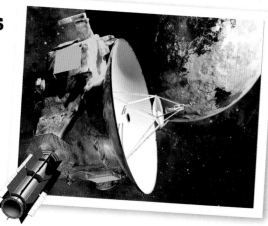

Fact file

» **Launch date:**
January 2006
» **Type of spacecraft:** Flyby
» **Size:** 8.9 ft (2.7 m) long
» **Mission status:** Ongoing

Hayabusa2 fired a bullet at the asteroid, uncovering rocks that were later collected.

Hayabusa2

This probe studied an asteroid close to Earth, called 162173 Ryugu. It sent rock samples back to Earth to help scientists understand the structure of asteroids. Hayabusa2 is now on its way to another asteroid, 1998 KY26.

Fact file

» **Launch date:**
December 2014
» **Type of spacecraft:**
Orbiter, Sample Return, Lander, and Rover
» **Size:** 5.2 ft (1.6 m) long
» **Mission status:** Ongoing

Lunokhod

The Lunokhod rover was a Soviet vehicle designed to travel across the surface of the moon. Lunokhod 1 became the first remote-controlled rover to successfully explore another object in space, taking photographs and studying the soil.

Fact file

» **Launch date:**
   November 1970
» **Type of spacecraft:**
   Uncrewed rover
» **Size:** 7.5 ft (2.3 m) long
» **Mission status:**
   Ended in 1973

Moon buggies

During America's Apollo 15, 16, and 17 moon missions, astronauts used lunar roving vehicles—nicknamed moon buggies—to explore the moon's surface from Earth.

Lunar roving vehicle

Lunokhod looked a little like a bathtub on wheels! Its tub-like body was for storing scientific equipment.

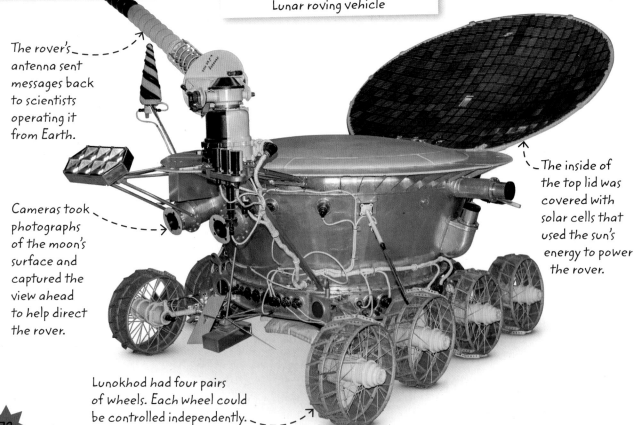

The rover's antenna sent messages back to scientists operating it from Earth.

Cameras took photographs of the moon's surface and captured the view ahead to help direct the rover.

The inside of the top lid was covered with solar cells that used the sun's energy to power the rover.

Lunokhod had four pairs of wheels. Each wheel could be controlled independently.

Curiosity Mars rover

Humans haven't made it to Mars yet, but we have sent robotic vehicles. One of the two largest is NASA's Curiosity, a car-sized rover. Sent to study the climate and surface of Mars, it carries equipment to collect and test rock samples.

THE BIGGEST PLANETARY ROVER

Mars landing

Unlike previous rovers, Curiosity was too heavy to use a parachute to float to Mars's surface. Instead, a spacecraft hovered above and the rover was lowered on a cable from a "sky crane."

Curiosity rover landing

Curiosity has seventeen cameras, including one with a laser that breaks up rocks on the surface to study them.

A robotic arm uses different tools to study the Martian rocks and soil.

Antennae receive instructions from Earth and send back information.

Powerful wheels help the rover trek across the bumpy ground.

Apollo

During the 1960s, the US space agency NASA developed the Apollo space program. Its aim was to send astronauts to the moon, and return them safely to Earth. Starting with Apollo 11 in 1969, six missions successfully landed on the moon.

» **Launch date:**
  February 1967
» **Type of spacecraft:**
  Lander and Orbiter
» **Size:** 36 ft (11 m) long
» **Mission status:**
  Ended in 1972

The cone-shaped command module had five windows. It was designed to carry three astronauts to the moon, then back to Earth.

The service module powered most of the spacecraft and held the main rocket engine and fuel tank. It also contained water and oxygen gas, which the astronauts needed to survive.

The top half of the lunar module carried two astronauts to the moon's surface. At the end of the mission, small engines fired to blast the spacecraft off the moon.

The lower half of the lunar module held the landing gear and scientific instruments. It was left on the moon.

Katherine was a mathematician at NASA.

Katherine Johnson

Johnson (1918–2020) calculated the path Apollo had to take to get to the moon from Earth. She also figured out the route needed for the lunar module to rejoin the command module once it left the moon's surface.

Soyuz

First launched in 1966, the Soyuz spacecraft was part of the Soviet Union's space program. The spacecraft's design is still used today, but with a few changes. It now takes crew and supplies to the International Space Station and back to Earth.

Fact file

» **Launch date:** April 1967 (first crewed flight)
» **Type of spacecraft:** Crewed spacecraft
» **Size:** 23.6 ft (7.2 m) long
» **Mission status:** Ongoing

Soyuz's first successful crewed mission was on October 26, 1968.

Apollo-Soyuz

In July 1975, the USA and the Soviet Union took part in the first international space mission. An Apollo spacecraft joined together with a Soyuz spacecraft. The crew shook hands, did science experiments, and exchanged gifts.

Two crewmembers of the joint USA-Soviet Union Apollo-Soyuz Test Project

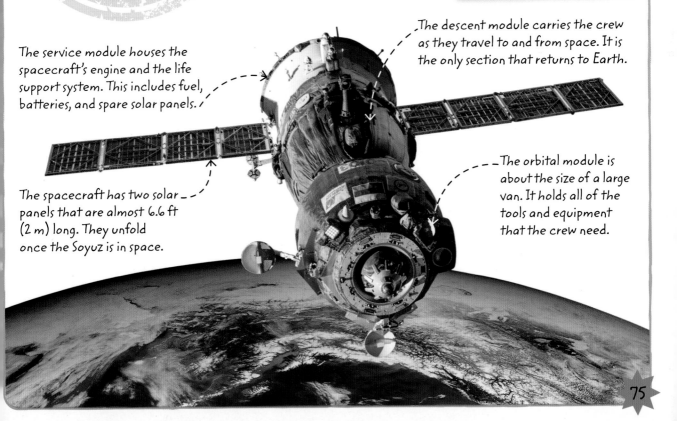

The service module houses the spacecraft's engine and the life support system. This includes fuel, batteries, and spare solar panels.

The descent module carries the crew as they travel to and from space. It is the only section that returns to Earth.

The spacecraft has two solar panels that are almost 6.6 ft (2 m) long. They unfold once the Soyuz is in space.

The orbital module is about the size of a large van. It holds all of the tools and equipment that the crew need.

Rockets

Rockets are vehicles that carry probes or crewed spacecraft into space. Their powerful engines burn fuel, blasting the rocket off the ground. Some rockets use solid fuel, while others use liquid. The fuel is stored in tanks inside the rocket.

Saturn V was taller than the Statue of Liberty in New York City!

Saturn V

The most powerful and successful rocket was Saturn V. It was built to send astronauts to the moon during the Apollo program. Saturn V had five rocket engines to give it a huge thrust into space.

Fact file

» **Launch date:** November 1967
» **Length:** 363 ft (111 m)
» **Agency:** NASA
» **Mission status:** Ended in 1973

Saturn V could carry up to 95,900 lb (43,500 kg)—the weight of six elephants—to the moon.

The first rockets were made in the 13th century in China.

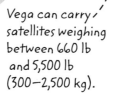

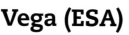

Vega can carry satellites weighing between 660 lb and 5,500 lb (300–2,500 kg).

Vega (ESA)

Vega is designed to put satellites into orbit around Earth, either at the poles or at its equator. It can carry multiple satellites in a single mission.

Fact file

» **Launch date:** February 2012
» **Length:** 98 ft (30 m)
» **Agency:** ESA
» **Mission status:** Ongoing

Long March 5

This is the world's third most powerful rocket. China used Long March 5 to launch probes to the moon and Mars. It will also be used to launch China's new space station.

Fact file

» **Launch date:** August 2001
» **Length:** 174 ft (54 m)
» **Agency:** JAXA
» **Mission status:** Ongoing

H-IIA (H-2A)

H-IIA has been used by the Japanese for more than forty-three launches since 2001, including the launch of a space probe to Mars and the Akatsuki spacecraft to orbit Venus.

Fact file

» **Launch date:** November 2016
» **Length:** 187 ft (57 m)
» **Agency:** CNSA
» **Mission status:** Ongoing

GSLV Mark III will launch a team of three astronauts into space in the Gaganyaan spacecraft.

Geosynchronous Satellite Launch Vehicle Mark III

GSLV Mark III is used by India to launch satellites into 24-hour orbits around Earth, meaning they stay in one spot over the planet as it rotates. The rocket helped to launch India's heaviest spacecraft, Chandrayaan-2, to the moon in 2019.

Fact file

» **Launch date:** June 2017
» **Length:** 142 ft (43 m)
» **Agency:** ISRO
» **Mission status:** Ongoing

Launch to re-entry

Since 1966, the Russian Soyuz spacecraft has been the most used in the world. Russia's rocket of the same name is used to launch the craft into space. In addition to SpaceX's Falcon 9 and Dragon, Soyuz is one of the only launchers to carry humans into space.

4

3

2

The casing protecting the spacecraft, called the fairings, falls away.

Launch
Astronauts experience weightlessness less than ten minutes after launching. It takes Soyuz around six hours to reach the space station.

1

The Soyuz spacecraft begins its journey to the ISS.

1. Liftoff
After years of planning and a final ten-second countdown, the engines fire up and reach full power in seconds. The rocket blasts into the sky.

2. Boosters detach
The four booster rockets burn for two minutes after liftoff, then fall away back to Earth.

3. Main tank empties
Five minutes after liftoff, the main tank, known as the first stage, runs out of fuel. It falls off, but a second fuel tank powers the Soyuz farther.

4. Docking
The second stage, or fuel tank, detaches and falls away. Soyuz docks with the ISS, allowing astronauts to board the space station.

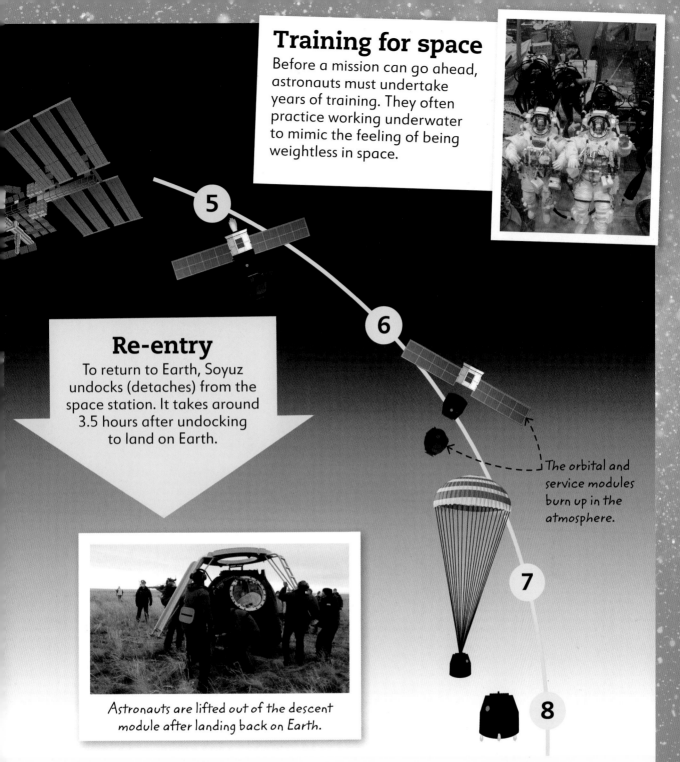

Training for space

Before a mission can go ahead, astronauts must undertake years of training. They often practice working underwater to mimic the feeling of being weightless in space.

5

Re-entry

To return to Earth, Soyuz undocks (detaches) from the space station. It takes around 3.5 hours after undocking to land on Earth.

6

The orbital and service modules burn up in the atmosphere.

7

8

Astronauts are lifted out of the descent module after landing back on Earth.

5. Undocking
Soyuz detaches from the ISS as the hooks connecting the craft to the space station are opened.

6. Modules separate
Three hours after undocking, modules used for living quarters and engines separate and fall away.

7. Parachutes open
As the descent module goes through the Earth's atmosphere, parachutes open to slow it down.

8. Landing
Two seconds before Soyuz hits the ground, six small engines fire to cushion the landing.

Shenzhou

China's Shenzhou spacecraft, meaning "divine craft," was designed to send taikonauts (Chinese astronauts) to space. Eleven spaceflights were launched in total, the first of which were test flights without a crew.

Fact file

» **Launch date:** November 1999
» **Type of spacecraft:** Uncrewed and crewed spacecraft
» **Size:** 30 ft (9 m) long
» **Mission status:** Ended in 200

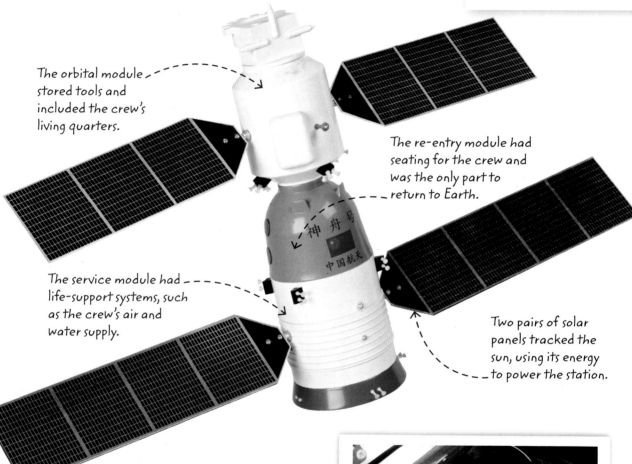

The orbital module stored tools and included the crew's living quarters.

The re-entry module had seating for the crew and was the only part to return to Earth.

The service module had life-support systems, such as the crew's air and water supply.

Two pairs of solar panels tracked the sun, using its energy to power the station.

First Chinese crewed flight

Yang Liwei was the first taikonaut in space, sent on the Shenzhou 5 mission in 2003. China became the third country to send a human into space, after the Soviet Union and the USA.

Yang Liwei

Space shuttle

US space agency NASA's space shuttle was the world's first partially reusable spacecraft. The orbiter (vehicle with wings) was launched by rockets and flew back to Earth when the mission was completed.

Fact file

» **Launch date:**
   April 1981
» **Type of spacecraft:**
   Crewed spacecraft
» **Size:** 121 ft (37 m) long
» **Mission status:** Ended in 2011

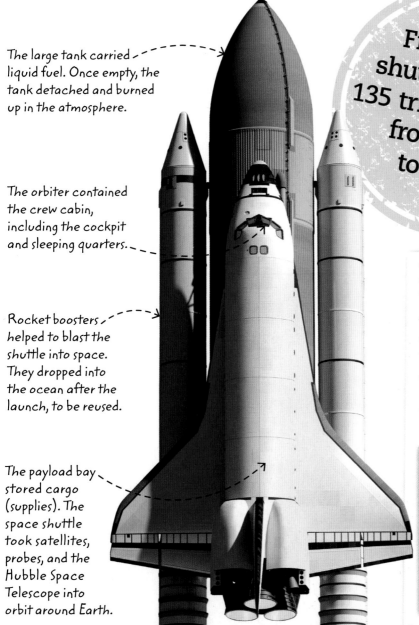

The large tank carried liquid fuel. Once empty, the tank detached and burned up in the atmosphere.

The orbiter contained the crew cabin, including the cockpit and sleeping quarters.

Rocket boosters helped to blast the shuttle into space. They dropped into the ocean after the launch, to be reused.

The payload bay stored cargo (supplies). The space shuttle took satellites, probes, and the Hubble Space Telescope into orbit around Earth.

Five space shuttles made 135 trips to space from 1981 to 2011.

Back to Earth

The space shuttle orbiter could land back on Earth like an airplane. It fired engines to slow down before landing. As the orbiter glided onto a runway, a parachute opened to slow it down further.

Space shuttle Discovery landing

81

Living in space

To live in space means living in microgravity, where everything floats and appears weightless. This presents challenges for astronauts, as well as for transporting enough air, water, and food from Earth.

In 2016, British astronaut Tim Peake was the first person to run a marathon in space.

The gym in the International Space Station (ISS) has many machines, including a treadmill.

Exercise

As astronauts float in space, their muscles and bones can weaken. They must exercise for around two hours each day to maintain their strength and stay healthy.

Sleeping

In space, astronauts are weightless, so they cannot lie down in a bed to sleep. Instead, they zip themselves up in sleeping bags inside their sleeping quarters—cabins the size of telephone booths.

If astronauts sleep outside their quarters, they can attach their sleeping bag to a wall.

Water often needs to be added to packaged food and it can also be heated in an oven.

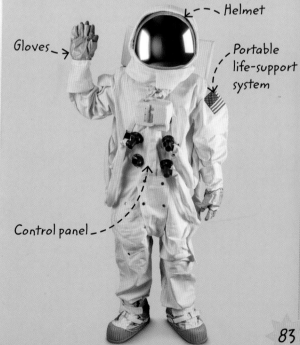

Food

Food for astronauts has to be tasty, healthy, and long-lasting. Food scientists design meals in sealed packages for spaceflight. The food cannot be crumbly, since it could float around and damage spacecraft equipment.

Working in space

Astronauts spend most of their time conducting science experiments and studying the effects of space on the human body. They also maintain the space station.

Space suit

Space suits protect astronauts from the airless environment of space, as well as from dust, temperature changes, and bright sunlight. They also hold many tools.

Helmet

Gloves

Portable life-support system

Control panel

Keeping clean

In space, water supply is limited. Astronauts use sponges and washcloths with a no-rinse cleaning solution to clean their hands and bodies. Most astronauts use edible toothpaste.

Astronauts wash their hair with water and no-rinse shampoo on the space station.

Mir

Mir was the first large space station with many modules, or sections. Launched by the Soviet Union (now Russia), it was built in space over ten years. Astronauts from twelve different countries visited Mir.

Fact file

» **Launch date:**
February 1986
» **Orbital period:**
92 minutes
» **Size:** 102 ft (31 m) long
» **Agency:** Soviet Union
(later Roscosmos)

STS-71 mission badge

The US space shuttle Atlantis docked with Mir in 1995, the first in a series of joint missions between the two countries.

Scientific experiments to monitor Earth took place in the Spektr module.

A special docking module helped the space shuttle attach to Mir.

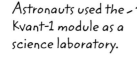

Astronauts used the Kvant-1 module as a science laboratory.

More solar panels were added to Mir to create additional power.

Early space stations

The first space stations launched into Earth's orbit were Salyut 1 by the Soviet Union and Skylab by the USA. Early stations were small and launched in one piece.

Skylab

A quail chick was the first animal born in space when it hatched on Mir in 1990.

84

International Space Station

Orbiting 250 miles (400 km) above Earth's surface, the International Space Station (ISS) is used as a science laboratory. Between three and six astronauts live on the ISS for months at a time, carrying out scientific research in space.

fact file

» **Launch date:** November 1998
» **Orbital period:** 93 minutes
» **Size:** 356 ft (108.5 m) long
» **Agency:** NASA, JAXA, Roscosmos, ESA, CSA

A 56 ft (17 m) long robotic arm helps move equipment and lift astronauts.

Science laboratory Kibo was added by Japanese agency JAXA.

NASA's Quest module stores space suits and has a door to exit the station.

Russia's Soyuz spacecraft brings astronauts and supplies to the space station.

The European Tranquility module contains bathrooms, gym equipment, and water storage.

International project

The ISS was made by the space agencies of America, Russia, Europe, Japan, and Canada. It has been visited by astronauts from eighteen countries.

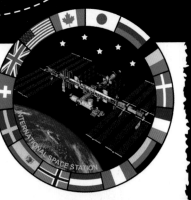

ISS logo

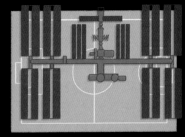

The ISS is approximately the size of a soccer field from end to end.

Future of space travel

Government agencies and private companies are building bigger and better spacecraft to explore our solar system and beyond. Uncrewed craft will continue to study planets, moons, and other objects in space. Astronauts will walk on the moon again and travel to Mars.

The first space tourist, Dennis Tito, visited the ISS in 2001.

Looking for life

Scientists will continue to look for life beyond Earth using newer and better equipment. Organizations such as the USA's SETI Institute look for advanced forms of life in space, which might be trying to communicate with us.

The Allen Telescope Array radio telescope in California is used for SETI searches.

Artemis program

Many years after Project Apollo, which put the first humans on the moon, NASA's Artemis program aims to allow humans to live on the moon for extended periods. NASA and its partners also plan to build a space station to orbit the moon.

Space tourism

As private companies develop spacecraft, they will soon be able to take people to space as safely as visiting another country on an airplane. Handfuls of tourists, such as Iranian-American Anousheh Ansari, have already visited space.

Going to Mars

NASA plans for humans to set foot on Mars in the 2030s. The first mission to Mars will spend around thirty to forty-five days on the surface, and astronauts will need to endure a two-year round trip to get there and back.

This image shows what life might be like for humans on Mars.

Anousheh Ansari

SpaceX Dragon

In May 2020, SpaceX Dragon—a partially reusable spacecraft—carried American astronauts Robert Behnken and Douglas Hurley to the ISS. SpaceX was the first private company to send people to space.

Fact file

» **Launch date:** March 2019 (uncrewed), May 2020 (crewed)
» **Type of spacecraft:** Crewed and uncrewed spacecraft
» **Size:** 14.4 ft (4.4 m) long
» **Mission status:** Ongoing

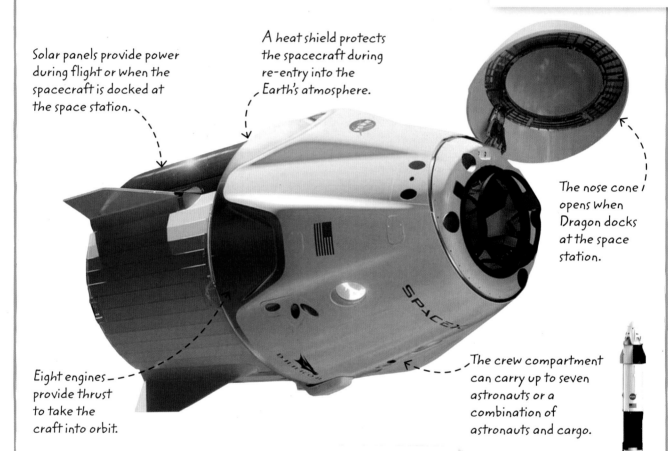

Solar panels provide power during flight or when the spacecraft is docked at the space station.

A heat shield protects the spacecraft during re-entry into the Earth's atmosphere.

The nose cone opens when Dragon docks at the space station.

Eight engines provide thrust to take the craft into orbit.

The crew compartment can carry up to seven astronauts or a combination of astronauts and cargo.

Private space companies

Bigelow Aerospace is one of many private companies aiming to send ordinary people to space. There are plans for spaceflights, hotels, and private modules on space stations.

Module by Bigelow Aerospace

Falcon 9 is a partially reusable rocket. The first stage booster detaches from the spacecraft after launch and lands vertically back on Earth.

Orion

NASA's new spacecraft, Orion, is partially reusable. It will take astronauts to the moon on the Artemis missions in the 2020s. Orion has everything the crew will need for up to twenty-one days.

Fact file

» **Launch date:**
December 2014
(test flight)
» **Type of spacecraft:**
Crewed spacecraft
» **Size:** 10 ft (3.3 m) long
» **Mission status:** Ongoing

Orion will safely carry astronauts to the moon and beyond.

The launch abort system will pull the spacecraft away from the rocket if there is a problem during launch.

The service module contains life-support systems that include things like water and oxygen.

The crew module safely carries up to four astronauts and forms their living space.

Four solar panels capture sunlight to provide power for the spacecraft.

Space Launch System (SLS)

Just slightly larger than Saturn V, the SLS is NASA's powerful new rocket that will be used for the Artemis program. It will also launch spacecraft deep into the solar system.

SLS rocket

All together

This book shows off some of the countless stars, planets, and space objects that have been discovered in our universe, along with important technology—new and old—used in space exploration.

The sun
pg. 18

Mercury
pg. 20

Venus
pg. 22

Earth
pg. 24

The Moon
pg. 26

Mars
pg. 28

Jupiter
pg. 30

Ganymede
pg. 32

Europa
pg. 33

Callisto
pg. 33

Io
pg. 33

Saturn
pg. 34

Iapetus
pg. 36

Enceladus
pg. 36

Titan
pg. 37

Hyperion
pg. 37

Uranus
pg. 38

Neptune
pg. 40

Pluto
pg. 42

Ceres
pg. 43

Vesta
pg. 46

Comet 67P/C-G
pg. 47

TRAPPIST-1e
pg. 48

51 Pegasi b
pg. 49

Milky Way
pg. 50–51

Pinwheel galaxy
pg. 52

**Small
Magellanic
Cloud**
pg. 53

Galaxy M87
pg. 53

Galaxy NGC 5866
pg. 53

**Orion
Nebula**
pg. 56

Eagle Nebula
pg. 57

Sirius
pg. 60

VY Canis Majoris
pg. 61

Orion
pg. 8

Ursa Major
pg. 9

Scorpius
pg. 10

Gemini
pg. 11

Cassiopeia
pg. 11

Crux
pg. 11

Atacama Large Millimeter Array
pg. 12

Canada-France-Hawaii Telescope
pg. 13

Lick Observatory
pg. 13

Paris Observatory
pg. 13

Hubble Space Telescope
pg. 62

Spitzer Space Telescope
pg. 63

Chandra X-Ray Observatory
pg. 64

INTEGRAL
pg. 65

Cassini-Huygens
pg. 70

Parker Solar Probe
pg. 70

Juno
pg. 71

New Horizons
pg. 71

Hayabusa2
pg. 71

Lunokhod
pg. 72

Curiosity Mars rover
pg. 73

Saturn V
pg. 76

Vega
pg. 76

H-IIA
pg. 77

Geosynchronous Satellite Launch Vehicle Mark III
pg. 77

Long March 5
pg. 77

Apollo
pg. 74

Soyuz
pg. 75

Shenzhou
pg. 80

Space shuttle
pg. 81

SpaceX Dragon
pg. 88

Orion
pg. 89

Mir
pg. 84

International Space Station
pg. 85

Glossary

asterism

recognizable pattern of stars found within a constellation

asteroid

object made of rock or metal that travels around the sun. Most asteroids are found in a band between Mars and Jupiter called the asteroid belt

astronaut

person who travels to space

astronomer

someone who studies the universe and everything in it

atmosphere

outer layer of gases surrounding most planets

axis

imaginary line running from the north pole to the south pole of an object, around which it spins

binary star

star system with two stars that orbit around each other

black hole

region of space where matter has collapsed in on itself. The gravity of a black hole is so strong that not even light can escape

cargo

equipment and supplies carried on spacecraft, such as food, water, scientific instruments, and spare parts

comet

object made of ice, rocks, and dust that orbits the sun

constellation

area of the sky containing a pattern of stars. There are eighty-eight internationally recognized constellations

core

ball-shaped central part of a planet, usually made of rock or metal

crew

group of people who travel to space together in a spacecraft

crust

outermost solid layer of a rocky planet

docking

joining of a spacecraft with a space station or another spacecraft in space

dwarf galaxy

small galaxy with only a few billion stars

equator

imaginary line around the center of a planet that divides it into a northern and southern hemisphere

gamma ray

most powerful form of light. Gamma rays are produced by the most energetic objects in the universe

gravity

force produced by an object, which pulls things toward its center

hemisphere

half of a round object, such as Earth

impact crater

large hole left in a planet or moon's surface by a fast-moving object, such as an asteroid, crashing into it

infrared light

invisible form of light that can be felt as heat energy and seen with special cameras

laboratory

room or building equipped for scientific experiments

lander

spacecraft that is designed to land on the surface of a planet or other space object

launch

when a spacecraft leaves Earth and reaches the speed in space at which it can remain in orbit

life-support system

part of a spacecraft or space suit that astronauts need to keep them alive in space, such as oxygen and water supply, and waste disposal

liftoff
the action of a spacecraft leaving the ground

light year
distance light travels in one year

lunar
relating to the moon

magnetic field
space around a planet that has a magnetic force

mantle
layer of a planet that sits between the core and the crust. The mantle is often the thickest layer of a planet

mass
the amount of material in a planet, star, or other space object

meteor
column of light left behind by a meteoroid when it breaks up on entering Earth's atmosphere

meteorite
piece of a space rock that has fallen to Earth

meteoroid
piece of rock or metal traveling through space

microgravity
condition in space in which gravity seems very weak. Microgravity is what causes astronauts and objects to appear weightless in space

module
self-contained part of a spacecraft or space station

molten
state of rock or metal when it becomes so hot it is no longer solid

nebula
huge cloud of gas and dust in space

orbiter
spacecraft that is designed to orbit a space object without landing on its surface

payload bay
part of the space shuttle orbiter that carries cargo

planetary nebula
stage of a dying star when it sheds its outer atmosphere and its hot core can be seen

planetary system
collection of one or more planets that orbits a central star in space

radio waves
least energetic form of light. A radio telescope is used to detect radio waves from distant stars and galaxies

re-entry
when a spacecraft re-enters the Earth's atmosphere from space

satellite
natural or man-made object that orbits a moon, planet, star, or galaxy

solar
relating to, or caused by, the sun

solar panel
panel made up of cells that convert sunlight into electricity

space walk
when an astronaut floats outside their spacecraft in space

spaceflight
journey to space

star-forming region
place in space where new stars are born

stellar
relating to stars

supernova
very bright explosion that happens when a massive star dies

Trojan asteroid
asteroid that shares its orbit around the sun with a larger object

ultraviolet light
invisible form of light that is given off by the sun and other stars

visible light
light rays that can be seen by the human eye

water ice
ice that is made up of water

water vapor
water in the form of a gas

weightlessness
feeling of floating that astronauts experience in space

X-ray
powerful form of light that is slightly less energetic than gamma rays. X-rays are given off by very hot objects in space

Index

51 Pegasi b 49

A

Aldrin, Buzz 67
Allen Telescope Array 87
Andromeda Galaxy 15, 52
animals in space 66
Ansari, Anousheh 87
Apollo missions/spacecraft 67, 72, 74, 87
Apollo-Soyuz Test Project 75
Armstrong, Neil 67
Artemis program 87, 89
asterism 9
asteroid belt 16, 43, 46
asteroids 5, 16, 20, 26, 43, 44, 46
astronauts 5, 66–67, 78–85, 86, 88–89
astronomy 6–7, 12–13
AstroSat 65
Atacama Large Millimeter Array (ALMA) 12
atmospheres 5, 19, 22, 23, 25, 29, 35, 38, 39, 41, 42, 43, 45, 49
auroras 19

B

balloon telescopes 65
Behnken, Robert 88
Big Bang 15
binary stars 60
black holes 50, 55, 61
blue stars 54, 58, 60
brown dwarfs 58

C

Callisto 33
Canada-France-Hawaii Telescope 13
Cassini-Huygens 70
Cassiopeia 11
Ceres 43, 44, 46
Chandra X-ray Observatory 64
Charon 42, 71
clouds 5, 22, 24, 31, 35, 38, 40, 56, 57

CNSA (China National Space Administration) 69, 77, 80
Comet 67P/Churyumov-Gerasimenko 47
comets 17, 45
command modules 74
constellations 6, 8–11
convective zone 19
cosmonauts 66–67
craters 20, 26, 42, 43, 46
Crux 11
CSA (Canadian Space Agency) 85
Curiosity Mars rover 73

D

Dawn spacecraft 43, 46
Deimos 28
descent modules 75, 79
docking/undocking 78–79, 84
Dragon spacecraft 78, 88
dwarf planets 17, 42–43

E

Eagle Nebula 57
Earth 5, 7, 14, 17, 23, 24–25, 26, 27
elliptical galaxies 52, 53
Enceladus 36
ESA (European Space Agency) 68, 76, 85
Europa 33
exercise in space 82
exoplanets 48–49
Explorer 1 66

FG

Falcon 9 78, 79
food in space 83
Gagarin, Yuri 66
galaxies 14–15, 50–51, 52–53
Galilei, Galileo 7, 32
Galileo spacecraft 30, 31
gamma rays 65
Ganymede 32
gas giants 17, 30–37
Gemini 11
Geosynchronous Satellite Launch Vehicle Mark III 77
Gidzenko, Yuri 67
Goldilocks zone 48
gravity 4, 5, 48

H

H-IIA 77
Halley's Comet 45
Hayabusa2 71
hemispheres, northern and southern 8–11, 51
Herschel, William 38
high-mass stars 54
Hubble Space Telescope 57, 62, 81
Hurley, Douglas 88
Hyperion 37

IJK

Iapetus 36
ice giants 17, 38–41
infrared light 62, 63
INTEGRAL (International Gamma-Ray Astrophysics Laboratory) 65
International Space Station 5, 67, 75, 78–79, 82, 85, 86, 88
Io 33
irregular galaxies 52, 53
ISRO (Indian Space Research Organisation) 65, 69, 77
JAXA (Japan Aerospace Exploration Agency) 77, 85
Johnson, Katherine 74
Juno 71
Jupiter 17, 30–31, 71
Kármán line 5
Kepler space telescope 49
Krikalev, Sergei 67
Kuiper Belt 17, 43, 44, 47, 71

L

La Silla Observatory 51
Laika 66
Large Magellanic Cloud 53
launch, rockets 78
lenticular galaxies 52, 53
Leonov, Alexei 67
Lick Observatory 13
life, extraterrestrial 87
life-support systems 75, 83
light years 14–15
living in space 82–83
Local Group 15
Long March 5 77
low-mass stars 54
luminosity 58
Luna 2 66
lunar modules 74
Lunokhod 72

M

magnetic fields 71
main sequence stars 58–59
Makemake 43
Mariner 4 67
Mars 17, 28–29, 67, 73, 77, 86, 87
mass 4, 18, 54, 58, 61
Mercury 17, 20–21
MESSENGER spacecraft 21
meteorites 45, 46
meteoroids 5, 45
microgravity 82
microwaves 65
Milky Way 14–15, 17, 50–51
Mir space station 84
Miranda 39
moon, the Earth's 26–27, 66, 67, 72, 74, 76 77, 86–87, 89
moons 5, 28, 30, 32–33, 36–37, 39, 40, 42
M87 53

N

NASA (National Aeronautics and Space Administration) 36, 43, 46, 68, 69, 73, 74, 76, 81, 85, 87, 89
nebulas 54, 56–57
Neptune 17, 40–41
Nereid 40
neutron stars 55
newborn stars 56
New Horizons 71
NGC 5866 53
North Star (Polaris) 9

O

observatories 12–13, 51, 63, 64
oceans 24, 28, 31, 32, 36
Oort Cloud 45
orbital modules 75, 79, 80
orbiters 81
orbits 4, 5, 7, 16
Orion 8
Orion Nebula 56
Orion spacecraft 89

P

Pan 36, 37
parachutes 79
Paris Observatory 13
Parker Solar Probe 70
Peake, Tim 82
Philae lander 47
Phobos 28
Pinwheel Galaxy 52
Pioneer spacecraft 19
planetary nebulas 55

planets 5, 14, 16–17, 20–41
Pluto 42, 71
private space companies 88

R

radio waves 12, 62
re-entry 79
re-entry modules 80
red dwarfs 59
red giants 55, 59
red supergiants 54, 59, 61
reusable spacecraft 81, 88–89
rings 30, 34, 38, 41
rockets 76–77, 78, 81, 88, 89
rocky planets 17, 20–29
Roscosmos 69, 84, 85
Rosetta spacecraft 47
rovers 72–73
Russia 67
    see also Roscosmos

S

Salyut 1 84
satellites 5, 66, 76, 81
Saturn 16, 17, 34–35, 70
Saturn V 76
Scorpius 10
service modules 74, 75, 79, 80, 89
SETI Institute 87
Shenzhou spacecraft 80
Shepard, Alan, Jr. 66
Shepherd, Bill 67
shepherd moons 37
Sirius A and B 60
Skylab 84
sleep in space 82
Small Magellanic Cloud 53
Sojourner rover 29
solar eclipses 27
solar power 18
solar system 7, 14, 16–47, 50, 51, 86
Soviet Union 66–67, 72, 75, 84
Soyuz spacecraft 75, 78–9, 85
Space Launch System (SLS) 89
space probes 70–1, 76, 77, 81
space race 66–7
space shuttle 81, 84
space stations 5, 82–5, 87
space suits 83
space telescopes 7, 62–3
space tourism 86, 87
space travel, future 86–87
space walks 67
SpaceX 78, 88
spiral galaxies 14, 15, 50–51, 52
Spitzer Space Telescope 63
Sputnik 1 66
star-forming regions 56, 57, 63
star life cycle 54–55

stars 5
stellar black holes 55
Stratospheric Observatory for Infrared Astronomy (SOFIA) 63
sun 4, 7, 14, 16, 18–19, 59, 70
supernovas 55, 59

T

telescopes 7, 12–13, 49, 62–65, 87
Tereshkova, Valentina 67
Titan 37, 70
Tito, Dennis 86
training, astronauts 79
TRAPPIST-1e 48
Triton 40, 41
Trojan asteroids 44

UVW

ultraviolet light 62, 65
United States 66–67, 84
    see also NASA
universe 14–15
Uranus 17, 38–39
Ursa Major 9
Vega 76
Venus 17, 22–23, 77
Vesta 46
visible light 62
volcanoes 22, 23, 24, 28, 33, 43
Voyager 1 and 2 35, 40, 70
VY Canis Majoris 61
washing in space 83
water 24, 32, 33, 36, 37, 41, 43, 47, 48, 49
weightlessness 78, 79, 82
white dwarfs 55, 58
White, Ed 67
working in space 83

XY

X-rays 64, 65
Yang Liwei 80
yellow dwarfs 16, 19, 59
yellow stars 54

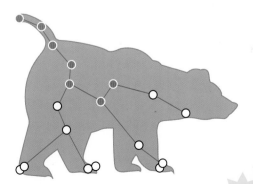

Acknowledgments

Dorling Kindersley would like to thank the following people for their assistance in the preparation of this book: Bettina Myklebust Stovne for illustration; Caroline Hunt for proofreading; and Helen Peters for the index.

The publisher would like to thank the following for their kind permission to reproduce their photographs:

(Key: a-above; b-below/bottom; c-center; f-far; l-left; r-right; t-top)

1–96 Dreamstime.com: Maximusnd (Border All Pages). **3 Dreamstime.com:** Nerthuz (tc). **Getty Images:** Martin Bernetti / AFP (b). **4 NASA. 5 Dreamstime.com:** Daveallenphoto (tc); Libux77 (crb). **NASA:** ESA, A. Simon (GSFC), M.H. Wong (University of California, Berkeley) and the OPAL Team (cr). **6 Alamy Stock Photo:** Art Collection 2 (cr); Alan Dyer / Stocktrek Images (tr). **6–7 Dreamstime.com:** David Herraez (b). **7 Alamy Stock Photo:** inga spence (br). **Dorling Kindersley:** Science Museum, London (cb). **Getty Images / iStock:** Hulton Archive (cr). **8 Science Photo Library:** John Sanford (bl). **9 Getty Images / iStock:** mycola (bc). **10 Science Photo Library:** Larry Landolfi (c). **12 Getty Images:** Martin Bernetti / AFP (b). **12–13 Dreamstime.com:** Andreistanescu (tc). **13 Alamy Stock Photo:** guichaoua (bl); Peace Portal Photo (cr). **14 Dreamstime.com:** Christos Georghiou (cb); Martin Holverda (bl). **14–15 NASA:** JPL-Caltech / R. Hurt (SSC / Caltech) (c). **15 Alamy Stock Photo:** Siloto (cr). **Dreamstime.com:** Martin Holverda (bl). **Science Photo Library:** Mark Garlick (t). **16 Alamy Stock Photo:** Photo Researchers / Science History Images (cb/Venus). **Dreamstime.com:** Archangel80889 (cb/Mars); Markus Gann (cl); Martin Holverda (cb/Earth); Dimitar Marinov (cra); Nerthuz (cr). **NASA:** Johns Hopkins University Applied Physics Laboratory / Carnegie Institution of Washington (cb). **17 Alamy Stock Photo:** Photo Researchers / Science History Images (cb/ Venus). **Dreamstime.com:** Nerthuz (cb/Jupiter). **ESA / Hubble:** Hubble & NASA, L. Lamy / Observatoire de Paris (cb). **NASA:** Johns Hopkins University Applied Physics Laboratory / Southwest Research Institute (cra); JPL-Caltech / T. Pyle (tl); JPL (cr, crb). **18 Dreamstime.com:** Markus Gann (c); Oxfordsquare (bc). **19 Getty Images / iStock:** Sjo (br). **20 NASA:** Johns Hopkins University Applied Physics Laboratory / Carnegie Institution of Washington; Johns Hopkins University Applied Physics Laboratory / Carnegie (bc). **21 NASA:** JHU / APL (br). **22 Alamy Stock Photo:** Photo Researchers / Science History Images. **NASA:** JPL-Caltech (bc). **23 NASA:** Venus (left): JPL, Magellan Project; Earth (right): Apollo 17 (br). **24 Dreamstime.com:** Martin Holverda. **26 Dreamstime.com:** Chiew Ropram (b). **NASA:** GSFC / Arizona State University. **27 Dreamstime.com:** Kdshutterman (b). **28 Dreamstime.com:** Archangel80889. **NASA:** (bc). **29 NASA:** JPL (bc); JPL-Caltech / UA (br). **30 Alamy Stock Photo:** NASA Image Collection (bc). **Dreamstime.com:** Nerthuz. **32 Alamy Stock Photo:** Tristan3D (b). **32–33 NASA:** JPL-Caltech / SETI Institute (tc). **33 Alamy Stock Photo:** Stocktrek Images, Inc. (br). **NASA:** JPL / DLR (tl, c). **34 Dreamstime.com:** Dimitar Marinov. **NASA:** JPL (br). **35 NASA:** JPL-Caltech / Space Science Institute (br). **36 ESA:** NASA / JPL-Caltech / University of Arizona / LPG / CNRS / University of Nantes / Space Science Institute (bc). **NASA:** JPL / Space Science Institute (cr). **37 NASA:** JPL-Caltech / Space Science Institute (tc, cr, bc); JPL / University of Arizona / University of Idaho (crb). **38 ESA / Hubble:** Hubble & NASA, L. Lamy / Observatoire de Paris (c). **Science Photo Library:** (bl). **39 NASA:** JPL / USGS (br). **40 Getty Images:** Corbis (bl). **NASA:** JPL (c). **41 Dreamstime.com:** Nerthuz (bl). **NASA:** JPL (br). **42 NASA:** Johns Hopkins University Applied Physics Laboratory / Southwest Research Institute (c, br). **43 Dreamstime.com:** Coatchristophe (bl). **NASA:** JPL-Caltech / UCLA / MPS / DLR / IDA (c). **Science Photo Library:** (br). **44 NASA:** (bl). **45 Alamy Stock Photo:** Art Directors & TRIP (tr). **46 NASA:** JPL / MPS / DLR / IDA / Björn Jónsson (c); JPL-Caltech (bc); University of Tennessee (br). **47 ESA:** ATG medialab (br); Rosetta / NAVCAM (c). **48 NASA:** JPL-Caltech (c). **49 NASA:** Ames / JPL-Caltech / T Pyle (cr); JPL-Caltech (c, bl, bc); Goddard / Francis Reddy (bc/Neptune). **50–51 Dreamstime.com:** Alexandr Mitiuc. **51 ESO:** José Francisco Salgado (josefrancisco.org) (cr). **NASA:** JPL-Caltech / ESA / CXC / STScI (crb). **52 NASA:** CXC / SAO (b); ESA; Z. Levay and R. van der Marel, STScI; T. Hallas; and A. Mellinger (cr). **53 ESA:** Gaia / DPAC, CC BY-SA 3.0 IGO (bc). **NASA:** ESA, and The Hubble Heritage Team (STScI / AURA) / W. Keel (University of Alabama, Tuscaloosa) (tr); ESA and the Hubble Heritage Team (STScI / AURA); Acknowledgment: P. Cote (Herzberg Institute of Astrophysics) and E. Baltz (Stanford University) (cl). **54 Alamy Stock Photo:** Diego Barucco (cb); Łukasz Szczepanski (crb). **Dreamstime.com:** Paweł Radomski (l). **NASA:** Solar Dynamics Observatory / Joy Ng (ca). **55 Alamy Stock Photo:** NASA Photo (clb). **NASA:** Goddard Space Flight Center (cr); NOAO, ESA, the Hubble Helix Nebula Team, M. Meixner (STScI), and T.A. Rector (NRAO) (ca); JPL-Caltech (crb). **56 Alamy Stock Photo:** Roth Ritter / Stocktrek Images. **ESA / Hubble:** NASA, L. Ricci (ESO) (br). **57 Alamy Stock Photo:** Roberto Colombari / Stocktrek Images; Łukasz Szczepanski (bc). **58 NASA:** JPL-Caltech / UCB (bl). **58–59 Alamy Stock Photo:** Ron Miller / Stocktrek Images. **60 Alamy Stock Photo:** Stocktrek Images, Inc. (bl). **NASA:** ESA, H. Bond (STScI) and M. Barstow (University of Leicester). **61 ESA / Hubble:** NASA / R. Humphreys (University of Minnesota) (c). **62 NASA:** (bc); Hubble (c). **63 Alamy Stock Photo:** Photo Researchers / Science History Images (clb). **Dreamstime.com:** Tanwalai Silp Aran (bl/clouds); Italianestro (bl). **64 Fotolia:** Natallia Yaumenenka / eAlisa (br). **NASA:** CXC & J.Vaughan (c). **65 ESA:** (c). **Indian Space Research Organisation:** (bl). NASA: (br). **66 Dreamstime.com:** Vitalii Gaydukov (cla). **Getty Images:** Sovfoto / Universal Images Group (tc). **NASA:** (crb). **Science Photo Library:** Qa International / Science Source (tc/Luna 1); Sputnik (tr); Detlev Van Ravenswaay (clb). **67 Alamy Stock Photo:** Pictorial Press Ltd (tl); SPUTNIK (tc). **NASA:** (cra, c, br); EVA (cl); JPL-Caltech (bl). **68 Alamy Stock Photo:** Liu Jie / Xinhua (cl). **ESA:** ATG medialab (tc). **68–69 Dreamstime.com:** Yehor Vlasenko. **69 Alamy Stock Photo:** Dinodia Photos (bl); ITAR-TASS News Agency (tl). **Dreamstime.com:** Alejandro Miranda (crb). **NASA:** (cra, fcra). **70 NASA:** Johns Hopkins APL / Steve Gribben (bl); JPL-Caltech (cr). **71 Alamy Stock Photo:** BJ Warnick / Newscom (b). **NASA:** JPL-Caltech (tl). **Science Photo Library:** NASA / Johns Hopkins University Applied Physics Laboratory / Southwest Research Institute (cr). **72 Dreamstime.com:** Aleks49 (b). NASA: (c). **73 NASA:** JPL-Caltech (b, cr). **74 Alamy Stock Photo:** Photo Researchers / Science History Images (cr). **75 Alamy Stock Photo:** Andrey Armyagov (b). **Getty Images:** Space Frontiers (cr). **76 Alamy Stock Photo:** Stephen Saks Photography (r). **ESA:** Jacky Huart, 2017 (bl). **77 Alamy Stock Photo:** ISRO / Xinhua (br); NG Images (tr). **Getty Images:** STR / AFP (tl). **78 Getty Images / iStock:** Vladimir Zapletin (cb). **79 NASA:** (tr); GCTC / Denis Derevtsov (clb). **80 Shutterstock.com:** Sipa (br). **81 Alamy Stock Photo:** NASA / Bill Ingalls (br). **Dreamstime.com:** Konstantin Shaklein. **82 NASA:** (cl, br). **83 123RF.com:** Fernando Gregory Milan (br). **Alamy Stock Photo:** NASA Photo (tr). **NASA:** (tl, tc, clb). **84 NASA:** (bc). **Science Photo Library:** NASA (cla). **85 NASA:** (bc). **86–87 NASA:** (t, bc). **87 Alamy Stock Photo:** BJ Warnick / Newscom (br). **Shutterstock.com:** Paulo Afonso (cra). **88 Alamy Stock Photo:** NASA Image Collection (bc). **Dreamstime.com:** Karaevgen (c). **Science Photo Library:** SPACEX (br). **89 NASA:** (br); ESA. **90 Alamy Stock Photo:** Roberto Colombari / Stocktrek Images (4:7); Photo Researchers / Science History Images (1:3); Tristan3D (1:8); Stocktrek Images, Inc. (2:3). **Dreamstime.com:** Archangel80889 (1:6); Markus Gann (1:1); Martin Holverda (1:4); Nerthuz (1:7); Dimitar Marinov (2:4); Alexandr Mitiuc (4:1). ESA: Gaia / DPAC, CC BY-SA 3.0 IGO (4:3); NASA / JPL-Caltech / University of Arizona / LPG / CNRS / University of Nantes / Space Science Institute (2:6); Rosetta / NAVCAM (3:6). **ESA / Hubble:** Hubble & NASA, L. Lamy / Observatoire de Paris (3:1); NASA, L. Ricci (ESO) (4:6). **NASA:** CXC / SAO (4:2); Johns Hopkins University Applied Physics Laboratory / Carnegie Institution of Washington (1:2); GSFC / Arizona State University (1:5); JPL / DLR (2:1, 2:2); JPL / Space Science Institute (2:5); JPL-Caltech / Space Science Institute (2:7, 2:8); JPL (3:2); Johns Hopkins University Applied Physics Laboratory / Southwest Research Institute (3:3); JPL-Caltech / UCLA / MPS / DLR / IDA (3:4); JPL / MPS / DLR / IDA / Björn Jónsson (3:5); JPL-Caltech (3:7, 3:8); ESA and the Hubble Heritage Team (STScI / AURA); Acknowledgment: P. Cote (Herzberg Institute of Astrophysics) and E. Baltz (Stanford University) (4:4); ESA, and The Hubble Heritage Team (STScI / AURA) / W. Keel (University of Alabama, Tuscaloosa) (4:5); ESA, H. Bond (STScI) and M. Barstow (University of Leicester) (4:8). **91 Alamy Stock Photo:** Andrey Armyagov (5:1); Peace Portal Photo (2:2); guichaoua (2:4); BJ Warnick / Newscom (3:6); Stephen Saks Photography (4:2); NG Images (4:4); ISRO / Xinhua (4:5). **Dreamstime.com:** Aleks49 (3:7); Andreistanescu (2:3); Konstantin Shaklein (5:3); Karaevgen (5:4). ESA: (3:1); Jacky Huart, 2017 (4:3). **ESA / Hubble:** NASA / R. Humphreys (University of Minnesota) (1:1). **Getty Images:** Martin Bernetti / AFP (2:1); STR / AFP (4:6). **NASA:** CXC & J.Vaughan (2:7); Hubble (2:5); JPL-Caltech (3:2, 3:4, 4:1); Johns Hopkins APL / Steve Gribben (3:3); ESA (5:5). **Science Photo Library:** NASA / Johns Hopkins University Applied Physics Laboratory / Southwest Research Institute (3:5). **92 Dreamstime.com:** Patrimonio Designs Limited (tr). **93 NASA:** (br). **94 Dreamstime.com:** Alexandr Yurtchenko (tc). **95 NASA:** JPL-Caltech (br). **96 Henry Leparskas:** (br)

Endpaper images: *Front:* **Alamy Stock Photo:** Photo Researchers / Science History Images tr, Stephen Saks Photography fcr, Tristan3D cla; **Dreamstime.com:** Aleks49 bc, Archangel8889 fcla, Karaevgen fcla (SpaceX), Libux77 cr, Dimitar Marinov tl; **ESA:** Jacky Huart, 217 ftl, ca (Integral), Rosetta / NAVCAM c (Comet); **NASA:** ca, Ames / JPL-Caltech / T Pyle cla (Kepler), CXC & J.Vaughan tc, Goddard / Francis Reddy c, Hubble fbr, Johns Hopkins University Applied Physics Laboratory / Carnegie Institution of Washington ca (Mercury), Johns Hopkins University Applied Physics Laboratory / Southwest Research Institute bc (Pluto), JPL ca (Neptune), JPL / DLR cl, JPL / MPS / DLR / IDA / Björn Jónsson clb, JPL-Caltech bl, crb, ftr; **Science Photo Library:** Qa International / Science Source fcra, Detlev Van Ravenswaay cl (Explorer 1 satellite), SPACEX tc (SpaceX); *Back:* **Alamy Stock Photo:** Photo Researchers / Science History Images tr, Stephen Saks Photography fcr, Tristan3D cla; **Dreamstime.com:** Aleks49 bc, Archangel8889 fcla, Karaevgen fcla (SpaceX), Libux77 cr, Dimitar Marinov tl; **ESA:** Jacky Huart, 217 ftl, ca (Integral), Rosetta / NAVCAM c (Comet); **NASA:** ca, Ames / JPL-Caltech / T Pyle cla (Kepler), CXC & J.Vaughan tc, Goddard / Francis Reddy c, Hubble fbr, Johns Hopkins University Applied Physics Laboratory / Carnegie Institution of Washington ca (Mercury), Johns Hopkins University Applied Physics Laboratory / Southwest Research Institute bc (Pluto), JPL ca (Neptune), JPL / DLR cl, JPL / MPS / DLR / IDA / Björn Jónsson clb, JPL-Caltech crb, bl, ftr; **Science Photo Library:** Qa International / Science Source fcra, Detlev Van Ravenswaay cl (Explorer 1 satellite), SPACEX tc (SpaceX);

Cover images: *Front:* **123RF.com:** solarseven crb; **Dreamstime.com:** Archangel80889 cra, Markus Gann bl, Konstantin Shaklein cl; **ESA:** NASA / JPL-Caltech / University of Arizona / LPG / CNRS / University of Nantes / Space Science Institute tr; **Getty Images:** STR / AFP cla; **Indian Space Research Organisation:** br; **NASA:** tc, ESA, A. Simon (GSFC), M.H. Wong (University of California, Berkeley) and the OPAL Team cb; *Back:* **Alamy Stock Photo:** Stephen Saks Photography cr; **Alamy Stock Photo:** Alexander Perepelitsyn bl; **ESA:** Rosetta / NAVCAM cb/ (Comet); **NASA:** Ames / JPL-Caltech / T Pyle cra, Hubble cla, JPL / DLR tr, JPL / MPS / DLR / IDA / Björn Jónsson c/ (Vesta), JPL / University of Arizona / University of Idaho bc, JPL-Caltech / Space Science Institute ca, University of Tennessee c, cb; **Science Photo Library:** Qa International / Science Source tl, Detlev Van Ravenswaay clb, SPACEX ftr

All other images © Dorling Kindersley
For further information see: www.dkimages.com

About the author

Dr. Parshati Patel is an astrophysicist, science communicator, and educator based in Canada. She develops space-themed programs for schools and the public, and often appears on TV and radio to talk about space. She also enjoys taking photos of the night sky.